Education, Music, and the Lives of Undergraduates

Also available from Bloomsbury

Activating Diverse Musical Creativities,
edited by Pamela Burnard and Elizabeth Haddon
Bloomsbury Handbook of Popular Music Education,
edited by Zack Moir, Bryan Powell and Gareth Dylan Smith
Quality in Undergraduate Education,
Monica McLean, Andrea Abbas and Paul Ashwin
Origins and Foundations of Music Education,
edited by Gordon Cox and Robin Stevens

Education, Music, and the Lives of Undergraduates

Collegiate A Cappella and the Pursuit of Happiness

Roger Mantie and Brent C. Talbot

BLOOMSBURY ACADEMIC
LONDON • NEW YORK • OXFORD • NEW DELHI • SYDNEY

BLOOMSBURY ACADEMIC
Bloomsbury Publishing Plc
50 Bedford Square, London, WC1B 3DP, UK
1385 Broadway, New York, NY 10018, USA
29 Earlsfort Terrace, Dublin 2, Ireland

BLOOMSBURY, BLOOMSBURY ACADEMIC and the Diana logo are
trademarks of Bloomsbury Publishing Plc

First published in Great Britain 2020
This paperback edition published in 2022

Copyright © Roger Mantie and Brent C. Talbot

Roger Mantie and Brent C. Talbot have asserted their right under the Copyright,
Designs and Patents Act, 1988, to be identified as Author of this work.

Cover design: Charlotte James
Cover image © Studio-Pro/ Getty Images

All rights reserved. No part of this publication may be reproduced or
transmitted in any form or by any means, electronic or mechanical, including
photocopying, recording, or any information storage or retrieval system,
without prior permission in writing from the publishers.

Bloomsbury Publishing Plc does not have any control over, or responsibility for,
any third-party websites referred to or in this book. All internet addresses given
in this book were correct at the time of going to press. The author and publisher
regret any inconvenience caused if addresses have changed or sites have
ceased to exist, but can accept no responsibility for any such changes.

A catalogue record for this book is available from the British Library.

Library of Congress Cataloging-in-Publication Data
Names: Mantie, Roger, author. | Talbot, Brent C., author.
Title: Education, music, and the lives of undergraduates : collegiate a cappella
and the pursuit of happiness / Roger Mantie and Brent C. Talbot.
Description: London ; New York : Bloomsbury Academic, 2020. |
Includes bibliographical references and index.
Identifiers: LCCN 2020033564 (print) | LCCN 2020033565 (ebook) |
ISBN 9781350169227 (hardback) | ISBN 9781350195714 (paperback) |
ISBN 9781350169234 (ebook) | ISBN 9781350169241 (epub)
Subjects: LCSH: Music in universities and colleges. | Choirs (Music)
Classification: LCC MT18 .M3 2020 (print) | LCC MT18 (ebook) | DDC 780.71–dc23
LC record available at https://lccn.loc.gov/2020033564
LC ebook record available at https://lccn.loc.gov/2020033565

ISBN:	HB:	978-1-3501-6922-7
	PB:	978-1-3501-9571-4
	ePDF:	978-1-3501-6923-4
	eBook:	978-1-3501-6924-1

Typeset by Integra Software Services Pvt. Ltd.

To find out more about our authors and books visit www.bloomsbury.com
and sign up for our newsletters.

For Susan

Contents

Foreword		viii
Preface		x
1	Staying Musically Active "I just can't ever imagine my life without music"	1
2	The Locus of Enjoyment "I like to be good, but not at the expense of happiness"	17
3	Gender and Sexuality in Collegiate A Cappella "A cappella goggles"	39
4	Sustaining Inequality through Singing "Your girlfriend will love us"	55
5	The Workings of Capital "If you are a legit institution, you probably have a cappella"	73
6	Agency and Amateurism "I feel like there's a stigma against anything recreational in music"	91
7	Future Orientations "I'm done with extreme music making"	111
8	Beyond Graduation "My mom looked at me and said, 'You need to sing!'"	123
References		142
Index		155

Foreword

I deleted the e-mail at first. It was the summer of 2015 and Bobby Cohen, Cornell Class of 1960, wanted my help. He was one of the earliest members of Cayuga's Waiters, Cornell's oldest all-male a cappella group, he explained, and he had a story to tell. More than fifty years after graduating, some of the original Waiters had started singing together again. They were in their seventies and eighties now and they'd been in touch sparingly, if at all. Most of these men hadn't seen each other in decades. Careers, marriages, children—it had all taken precedence.

But then, just like that, Charlie Wolfe '55 had sent out a letter, asking if the old gang would like to get together again? What started as a one-time gathering at the Basin Harbor Club on Lake Champlain turned into an unlikely annual tradition, and then something even more surprising: Starting in 2005 or 2006, Bobby told me, these men would descend on Ithaca, New York, for Cornell's Reunion Weekend, where they'd frantically rehearse five or six old songs and perform at brunches and lunches and even on stage at Bailey Hall (a massive arena on campus). They'd even sleep in the dorms again—enduring communal showers and stifling heat all in the name of a cappella singing.

Bobby wanted to know: Would I like to make a documentary about them? I knew why he'd reached out to me. I had some experience in the area. My non-fiction book, *Pitch Perfect*, about the competitive world of a cappella singing, had inspired the movies of the same name. Also, I'd been a Waiter myself, albeit forty years after Bobby graduated. Still, I tried to say no. I had a quick phone call with Bobby—a courtesy, really—explaining that I'd recently moved to Los Angeles and was busy with other projects. I even tried to pawn the idea off on a friend of mine, Zachary Weil, a younger Waiter alum who was making documentaries and corporate films.

But in the weeks that followed, I couldn't stop thinking about Bobby's story. In part because of what he'd said but also because the dude was relentless! He followed up by e-mail from his home in Bethlehem, Pennsylvania, to put a fine point on this journey. "What's compelling about this story?" he wrote, before immediately answering his own question: "The power and joy of collaborative singing, how it endures throughout lifetimes, brings people together of different backgrounds and opinions (yes, there are lots of Republicans in this group, and Navy veterans, and nobody who made a living as a singer, but a few who tried)."

He finished with a plea disguised as a question: "Does what I've said here give you an idea of what we might make of this?"

I couldn't believe I was saying this but: Yes, it had. What finally hooked me was simple: I imagined what it might feel like to be seventy-five years old and going back to college again. What Bobby was talking about wasn't just a human interest story or "Pitch Perfect" for old people. It was the Fountain of Youth. I called him to say: "I'm in."

Zack and I teamed up together. And in the lead-up to June 2016—the group's next reunion—we took a bunch of road trips to interview some of these men on camera. We sat in their living rooms in Connecticut and Pennsylvania and Illinois, hearing wild stories about the Waiters in the group's heyday—about how they'd performed live on TV's "The Perry Como Show," about how they would show up unannounced at a women's college to serenade the co-eds, about how they toured the world and recorded vinyl records and created a tradition I was lucky enough to join as a freshman at Cornell in 1996. Actually, that's a lie. I didn't get into the group until I was a sophomore. They made me audition four times before they finally accepted me—or took pity on me. I don't care which it was. Because those friendships changed my life.

When Reunion Weekend finally arrived, Zack and I drove to Ithaca (along with a second camera operator we'd hired) and moved into the dorm alongside The Waiters of the 1950s, as they called themselves. The mattresses may have been thin—as were the walls—but our hearts were full. In rehearsal, these liver-spotted singers argued like teenagers. Late at night, after performing, they partied like them too, gathering in the dorm lounge to have a drink and sing some more. When they took to the stage for the finale on Saturday night—dressed up in navy jackets and striped ties—to perform for 1,600 Cornellians, I had to fight back tears.

Bobby Cohen was maybe the youngest member of this group. And so, it was a shock when, on December 6, 2016—shortly before Zack and I finished the film—Bobby died suddenly at his home. He was seventy-eight. We were devastated. I went back to find that first e-mail he'd written. And damn if he hadn't warned me. "We keep doing it," he wrote, "year after year. And the Grim Reaper lessens our ranks little by little."

Our short documentary—a love letter to the Waiters of the 1950s—played a bunch of film festivals across the country in 2017. We called the movie *Old Men Singing*. The title was meant to be a joke. But when I look back on it now, I think it's why we made the movie. And—in a way—why Roger and Brent wrote this book. Old men singing? We should be so lucky.

Mickey Rapkin, February 21, 2020

Preface

Even the busiest among us have *some* discretionary time. What we choose to do with that time is both a product of our upbringing and a reflection of who we think we are and wish to be. The college (or "university"[1]) years are often pivotal in this regard because this point in one's life typically represents the first opportunity to make decisions over the use of discretionary time independent of parental authority. For some, this might mean partying to one's heart's content. For others, it might mean playing video games for hours on end (without those pesky parental control time limits). For still others, the college years represent the chance to join a religious club, a sports club, a drama club, or, perhaps, an a cappella group.

The idea of joining an a cappella group for the purpose of singing signals a commitment that places the activity in contrast to the kind of informal, casual singing that, for hundreds of years, used to characterize American college campuses (Winstead 2013). It is actually a bit misleading to suggest one simply "joins" an a cappella group. One *auditions* in the hopes one is accepted. There is a kind of exclusivity to a cappella that marks participants as special. They are *the chosen*. Significant also is that a cappella as a student "club" is distinguishable from a campus's institutionally led choirs. This isn't just singing. This is singing as governed and managed by the participants themselves. Historically, "collegiate" a cappella (as opposed to simply "a cappella") arose in the early twentieth century as a pushback against the "formal" music offerings on campus led by trained "conductors" who invariably imposed their conception of "right" music done the right way. Collegiate a cappella was, and is, about the empowered *student voice.*

We are not the first to write about collegiate a cappella. Mickey Rapkin's (2008) *Pitch Perfect* (the book upon which the movie franchise is based) and Joshua Duchan's (2012a) *Powerful Voices: The Musical and Social World of Collegiate a Cappella*, an ethnographic examination of three Boston area collegiate a cappella groups, are both excellent sources for the history and context of collegiate a cappella and provide wonderful insights into a cappella *qua* a cappella. In the trade publishing world, Deke Sharon (who Rapkin calls

---

[1] Following American practice, we use college and university more or less interchangeably.

"the father" of collegiate a cappella) has written several books on a cappella, often with an aim of promoting and supporting the practice (e.g., *So You Want to Sing A Cappella: A Guide for Performers*). On the scholarly side, there are some conference presentations, theses, dissertations, and journal articles (Alberti 2017, Baird et al. 2018, Berglin 2018, 2015, Burlin 2015, Duchan 2007, 2012b, Haning 2019, Paparo 2013, St. Jean 2014, Slutsky 2005, Griffin 2017, Stewart 2016) that examine various aspects of collegiate a cappella—or, as is now the more fashionable and inclusive way of describing it: *contemporary* a cappella. There is even a handbook as part of a widely used pedagogical series for school music: *Teaching Music through Performance in Contemporary A Cappella*.

So why a(nother) book on collegiate a cappella? *Why this—why now?* For starters, we live in neoliberal times where the idea of students spending time on any "non pre-professional activity" (as one of our informants put it) is considered irrational at best, irresponsible at worst. That thousands of college students, including those pursuing "intense" courses of study at the world's top universities, spend countless hours singing rather than studying would seem to challenge the belief that all people have been reduced to human capital at the mercy of global commerce. This alone seems sufficiently provocative to justify deeper investigation. Beyond the neoliberal critique, however, we are both educators committed to the idea that making music "avocationally" (recreationally, for leisure, etc.) throughout one's life is a pretty healthy thing to do. That so many non-music majors involve themselves of their own volition in a student-run, time-consuming, non-credit activity at such a critical (liminal?) point in their lives seems to us a rather remarkable phenomenon. Perhaps the field of music learning and teaching might glean something from studying those who choose to make music when they don't have to—especially those who find a way to do it independent of a musical "expert"?

About the Book

This book started out as a small-scale investigation intended as a journal article. It turned out to be a nine-year (2010–2019) study of collegiate a cappella (63 informants, 24 groups at 14 campuses). The "matters of concern" in this book reflect our backgrounds as music education professors with a passion for and interest in advancing broad-based understandings of musical participation in society. Rather than studying the phenomenon of collegiate a cappella itself (as is the case with Duchan's work or Rapkin's work, for example), we focus more on singing as a social practice as part of people's lives, where recreational involvement during the college years is set against the context of a larger life course.

In the vein of Thomas Turino's *Music as Social Life* and Lucy Green's *How Popular Musicians Learn*, this book takes an ethnomusicological and sociological approach to research. Due to the range of issues examined in the book, readers may be interested in some chapters more than others (although we would like to think everyone will enjoy it cover to cover). Our research focuses less on the practice of creating and singing in a collegiate a cappella group and more on how collegiate a cappella participation might shed light on issues of gender, sexuality, diversity, class, musical agency, and lifelong musical participation. Throughout the book we engage scholarship from a range of disciplines, though admittedly we lean more sociological than psychological.

One of our aims while writing the book was to produce a text that was theoretically rigorous yet broadly accessible. We have adopted a (mostly) conversational tone and woven the empirical data throughout the discussion to allow the informants' voices to sing through as much as possible–going as far as to use their words as subtitles for every chapter. That said, we are very much aware that "data" do not speak for themselves. Although we have concentrated much of the "theory" in Chapters 4–6, theoretical considerations informed our writing of every chapter.

Many researchers are rightly concerned with "method," wanting an explanation and justification for each and every decision made in the collection and analysis of the data. We have provided some general details throughout the book but, in the interest of readability, have left out much of what might be expected of a study appearing in a peer-reviewed research journal. For those interested, our approach might be described as qualitative with phenomenological leanings. Consistently with what might be loosely termed an ethnographic approach, we embraced the phenomenon naturalistically. Although some might be tempted to label what we have done as "grounded theory," this isn't how we approached the study. Our theoretical biases (e.g., Bourdieu, Butler, Foucault) preceded our investigation. We have used theory to help make meaning of the empirical data; we have not attempted to "do theory."

To put it in the language of research, the "unit of analysis" of this study can be considered *lifestyle* (cf. Weber) insofar as we were interested in understanding how those involved with collegiate a cappella "made sense" of recreational music making within the context of their educational experience while at university and how they placed it within the broader contexts of their lives. As described in more detail in the book, the informants were drawn from a convenience sample, with Roger's work involving multiple groups at multiple sites to provide breadth and Brent's work involving concentrated, sustained involvement with a group to provide depth. Our observations of the groups (in rehearsal and performance)—though in Roger's case only "one-offs"—served to provide context for the interviews. The interviews themselves tended to be around an hour in length.

The interview protocol included many questions to generate contextual information about the participants. Most of this does not appear in the book. For example, we inquired about where they grew up, what year they were currently completing in their undergraduate trajectory, what major they were pursuing, if music was an integral part of their home life, whether their parents or siblings were musically active, when they first started making music and their reasons for starting music, whether they participated in school music and what they remember from their elementary and secondary school classes, and if they participated in music making outside of elementary and secondary school. We also inquired about the role competition played in their musical lives, how they approached learning music, the types of ensembles and music-making experiences they participated in outside of a cappella, and what they felt they learned most from their experiences in a cappella.

With field notes from twenty-four groups and interviews with sixty-three informants, we had a *lot* of data. We began with "in vivo" coding, compiling the codes and categories into two (rather massive) multi-tabbed Google sheets. We met at least two hours, sometimes eight hours, almost every week for over six years via video chat, during which time we painstakingly continued to label and categorize the data, re-listening to interviews to verify context, tone, and meaning. Over this time, the chapters began to take shape. Although we conducted an initial literature review before embarking on the study (back when this was to be just a journal article), we continued to read and discuss literature in order to put it in conversation with our data. Although the primary data collection period was 2010–2015, we continued to collect data on undergraduates right up to 2019. We also conducted some follow-up interviews in 2019 with some of our original interviewees from 2011–2013. This proved invaluable in providing the opportunity to constantly reflect on our analysis while in the process of writing the book.

* * *

When we initiated this project, we thought—naïvely perhaps—that this was going to be a simple study about lifelong music making and its connections with school music learning and teaching. About a year into the research, however, we realized that such a restricted scope failed to reflect the complexities involved. *Singing is never just singing.* Our original title for this book was *Beneath the Covers: Dedication, Desire and Distinction on Campus*. We thought it clever because of the double entendre of "beneath the covers." (The genre of collegiate a cappella is about "covering" pop songs.) We felt it reflected how we explore the social complexities of what goes on "beneath" the superficial sheen of imitating radio hits with voices alone, *and* discuss issues of gender and sexuality in collegiate a cappella. *Perfect!* We also thought the subtitle alluded to the Butlerian aspects of performativity in Chapter 4 and captured the Bourdieusean theoretical framework we use in Chapter 5. Unfortunately, our title was just a bit too clever. In retrospect we realize that a good title in 2020 owes the reader just a little bit more insight into the content of the book. (It seems to have escaped our notice that our original title fails to mention music or singing, and seems to imply a campus-wide investigation of sexual practices.)

Education, Music, and the Lives of Undergraduates: Collegiate A Cappella and the Pursuit of Happiness is a title intended to reflect the most salient aspects of the book's content and delimit what the book is *not* about. This book isn't really about a cappella, for example. We aren't musicologists; we didn't analyze arrangements or choreography or vowel production. Instead, this is a book about the *meaning* that this particular form of singing holds for college students in the broader context of their lives, particularly in relation to their education.

Students go to college on the pretense of *learning* as part of degree attainment. They also have an expectation of extra-curriculars (*leisure*) that constitute a major part of the "college experience." As is evident throughout, but especially in our final chapter, collegiate a cappella helps to forge lasting friendships and relationships that leave an indelible mark on all of its participants. At the same time, however, collegiate a cappella also enacts and sustains multiple forms of privilege and inequality through its audition practices and its performative enactment of gender and heteronormativity. This book raises many questions about the role of leisure, especially leisure-time music making, during the college years and in the broader context of people's lives.

Although we have not explicitly considered recreational college singing beyond the United States and Canada, we have little reason to believe that college/university students in other countries differ substantially in the way they approach learning and leisure. In an interconnected, global world, we believe the issues raised in this book hold broad implications that transcend the geographic contexts of the data collection. That said, all things are contextual. We have done our best to qualify our discussions throughout the book by including adjectives like "American" or "American and Canadian," but, in the interest of not weighing down the prose, have entrusted the reader to apply interpretive judgment as appropriate.

About Us

As music education professors, the two of us came to the world of collegiate a cappella from very different places. Roger, a jazz and classical saxophonist, spent many years as a high school band director in Canada. From 2009 to 2014, Roger worked at Boston University, where his responsibilities included leading small jazz groups for non-music majors. Early in his first semester at Boston University, he learned that one of the members couldn't make a particular rehearsal due to a conflict with her "a cappella group." Roger mistakenly thought this was a formal music group in the College of Fine Arts. Only after some discussion did he come to learn about this phenomenon so prevalent in the US northeast (collegiate a cappella groups exist beyond the US northeast, extending even to some Canadian universities, but they are not nearly as omnipresent as they seem to be in the northeastern United States). Given his research interests in recreational and lifelong music making, he considered collegiate a cappella to represent an opportunity to learn more about how people volitionally involve themselves in music making independent of an official "expert" or authority figure. Conveniently, the Greater Boston area is replete with colleges and universities affording access to dozens and dozens of collegiate a cappella ensembles. Roger's subsequent academic appointments at Arizona State University (2014–2018) and University of Toronto (2018–present) provided the opportunity to further explore collegiate a cappella in a setting far removed from the US northeast and its Ivy League history.

Brent's formative experiences help to explain the interest in this book. Brent attended Indiana University as an undergraduate and was a classmate of members of *Straight No Chaser*, an a cappella group that has since parlayed its origins as a student-led group into an award-winning, multi album, touring group with over 23 million views on YouTube. As witness to the development and interest of collegiate a cappella in the mid- to late 1990s, Brent regularly attended his classmates' shows and observed firsthand the obsessed fan-following that these groups generated. As a music education major, he was curious as to how this student-led music-making experience could pack auditoriums on campus, while some of the most outstanding musicians at one of the top music schools in the world were struggling to fill recital halls on campus. This curiosity led him in graduate school and beyond to examine the discourses surrounding music performance and learning practices in and out of school settings. Serendipitously, within his first few weeks as a new professor at Gettysburg College, Brent was asked to be the faculty advisor to the all-male a cappella group on campus. The group was interested solely in having Brent be an advisor on paper—a requirement for any group looking to receive funding from the student senate.[2] As a music faculty member, however, Brent only agreed if the members would allow him to coach and spot-check their work prior to any performance.

The two of us were introduced (c. 2010) by the late Susan Conkling, who suggested to each of us that we would benefit from working together based on our shared interests. Indeed, our shared theoretical grounding in poststructuralism, mainly Foucault, provided a launching point for a number of research projects (c. 2011–2015) that examined structures of participation and social reproduction in music education (Mantie and Talbot 2015, Talbot and Mantie 2015). Our interrelated concerns about the "state of music education" had us considering why and how people participate in music throughout their lives—whether in spite of or because of their school music education experiences.

After a year of observing collegiate a cappella groups and interviewing members, Roger realized that the richness of this phenomenon exceeded the typical boundaries of a journal-style research study. He also recognized that in order to bring greater "insider" knowledge (an "emic" perspective, in ethnographic terms) to his "outsider" (etic) perspective as an instrumentalist, he needed to collaborate with someone more immersed in the vocal world. Given his existing research activities and relationship with Brent, a choral educator who just happened to be a faculty advisor for a collegiate a cappella group, it was a match made in heaven. As a choral educator, Brent's interpretive frame was decidedly more intimate and accounted for a more nuanced knowledge of the actors involved. Roger's observations and interviews, on the other hand, involved a wider range of groups and individuals from a variety of institutions in the US northeast (and a small number in the US southwest and Canada), but were, with a few exceptions, single-contact. From a research perspective, the balance of our insider and outsider views proved invaluable in making sense of the "data," in that many nuances could be figured out and balanced against temptations to overgeneralize.

---

[2] Most a cappella groups do not have faculty advisors, except in cases where this is a requirement for recognition as an official campus organization. In most of these instances the role is nominal.

With Thanks

As individuals sensitive to research ethics, we struggled tremendously with our motives and research practices throughout this endeavor. Regardless of the altruistic motives involved in "contributing to research," it cannot be dismissed that researchers advance their careers thanks to the volunteerism of participants. We recognize and appreciate that virtually all unfunded "human subjects" research involves an asymmetrical relationship, but this fact does little to alleviate our guilt. The demands for anonymity common among university institutional review boards in the United States, done understandably in the name of protecting research "subjects," removes the possibility of properly acknowledging the donation of time and energy given by the individuals who accepted our interview and observation requests.

For purposes of clarity and respect we have used the term "informants" (and "interviewees" in Chapter 8) rather than "participants" to describe those whom we interviewed. First, this makes it easy to discuss all those involved in collegiate a cappella as *participants* (versus the "informant" subset we interviewed), and second, it acknowledges that the individuals we interviewed *informed* our research by answering our questions; to call them participants is to disingenuously imply they had a more active, participatory role in the research. In lieu of naming individuals (we use pseudonyms throughout), we list here, with our sincerest gratitude, the names of all the groups whose members indulged our interviews and observations:

Allegrettos	*PowerChords*
Aural Fixation	*Priority Male*
BC Dynamics	*Ramifications*
BC Sharps	*sQ!*
Choralaries	*Surround Sound*
Company B	*Terpsichore*
Drop the Octave	*The Dear Abbeys*
FourScores	*The Nor'Easters*
Heard on the Street	*Tupelos*
In Achord	*UniSons*
LowKeys	*VoiceMale*
MIT/Wellesley Toons	*Wellesley Widows*

1
Staying Musically Active

"I just can't ever imagine my life without music"

Setting the Stage

It is 11:00 PM on a crisp spring Sunday night. Roger has been observing a rehearsal of an a cappella group in a medium-sized classroom on the campus of one of the world's great science and technology universities—one that offers a few music classes but otherwise does not have a "school" of music. Someone in the group has arranged, notated, and printed out a song heard frequently on the radio. The students, primarily mathematics and engineering majors, have been rehearsing the song for close to an hour. The group regularly rehearses until midnight (or later), but Roger has an early morning and still has to drive home. He sneaks out and closes the door behind him. As he walks toward the end of the building, he passes a classroom with another a cappella group, and next to it he passes yet another...

On almost any college campus in the United States of America one can find a small group of people gathered, often late in the evening, singing unaccompanied music, usually for several hours at a time. These groups typically consist of about twelve to fifteen students (not coincidentally a number that can fit in a fifteen-passenger van). One can occasionally find in such groups a music major or two, especially if the university has a music school, but the majority of students in these singing groups come from all parts of campus. Most have had prior ensemble singing experiences, either in school or elsewhere, but for some, this may be their first involvement in a singing group. Their musical backgrounds and training vary from intense instrumental study to nothing beyond singing in the shower.

If understood simply as unaccompanied group singing, *a cappella* may be one of the oldest forms of musical activity in the world. From its more formalized religious origins and its manifestations as barbershop and doo-wop, a cappella singing has benefited logistically (and economically) from its sole reliance on the human voice. One requires only a group of people willing to sing; no other equipment needs to be procured and almost any space will do. While formal training and/or diligent practice may increase the sophistication of the repertoire or technical performance level, the point of entry for participation remains accessible to almost anyone with a desire to sing.

Many people in the United States are familiar with a cappella singing due to the popularity of the television series *Glee* (though often the singing on the show wasn't, strictly speaking, a cappella), the televised contest *The Sing-Off*, the *Pitch Perfect* movies, and the group Pentatonix. "Collegiate" a cappella, for those less familiar, is a musical practice on college (university) campuses arising from a wider glee club movement in the early twentieth century that witnessed an upsurge in recreational singing. While a cappella singing on higher education campuses was hardly unprecedented in the late nineteenth and early twentieth centuries (see Winstead 2013), a strong feature of collegiate a cappella (in common with barbershop singing) is its decidedly grassroots, amateur aesthetic, something witnessed on multiple fronts, but perhaps signaled most obviously in the pun-infused group names (e.g., Treblemakers, Aural Fixation, Priority Male).

In many ways, collegiate a cappella epitomizes ensemble-based recreational, volitional music making. Rather than rely on the musical direction and organization of an established "expert" (i.e., a conductor employed by the institution), an underlying feature of collegiate a cappella was and is that groups were/are typically self-run, relying on the musical skills and abilities existing among group members. Due to its scheduling convenience (outside of class hours) and independence from curricular structures, collegiate a cappella has provided, and continues to provide, opportunities for thousands of students who wish to remain musically active during their college years. "Michelle" and "Zach" are two such students. At the time of our study, Michelle was a first-year biomedical engineering major at a large urban research university; Zach was a first-year environmental studies major at a small, rural liberal arts college.

Michelle

Raised in southern New Jersey, Michelle started playing the piano in second grade and began singing in school in sixth grade. Her parents did not participate in music themselves, but her grandmother had "the voice of an angel." Michelle's parents were not demanding but supportive enough to invest in a grand piano.

In middle school she took up the trombone, eventually switching to the bass trombone, and joined jazz band in ninth grade—an interest fueled in part by watching the Ken Burns jazz series courtesy of her grandmother.

Music was important to Michelle, especially in her high school years, where she was widely known for her music. Music wasn't her sole activity, however. She painted (oils, pastels), played tennis regularly (which kept her from participating in marching band), and was seriously involved in dancing (both ballet and tap) through her senior year in high school. Looking back, she thought it was perhaps weird for a thirteen- to fourteen-year-old to love jazz and Fred Astaire so much.

Despite her accomplished piano and trombone skills, Michelle really loved to sing. To her disappointment, however, she was never accepted into the school choir. The chorus director encouraged her to audition every year, saying, "Try out; you'll get in," but he never accepted her into the group. "He would always get my hopes up for the musical and the chorus," she lamented, "but in the end... " For the school musicals she tried out every year but was accepted only for dancing roles. In her senior year she decided not to audition for the chorus. In response, the chorus director accused her of being a quitter. Her relationship with the school's band director, on the other hand, was very strong. He was, quite simply, "the best."

Michelle thought about doing a music minor at university but realized that the courses and scheduling would be next to impossible with her biomedical engineering major. Her university applications were thus influenced very strongly by her research into schools that would afford her opportunities to continue making music, both jazz and singing, as a nonmajor or nonminor. Her final list of university applications was remarkably small.

Even though she always thought that a cappella singing (of any style or genre) was "the coolest thing in the world," Michelle never had the opportunity to participate in such groups. As a result, when she attended the university's activity fair, she was hesitant to approach the a cappella groups. To her pleasant surprise, the student singing groups saw great potential in her. She got callbacks from three groups and was accepted into two of them. She was also accepted into the jazz combo program as both a pianist and vocalist, where she quickly became regarded as the premiere solo vocalist due to her fantastic sense of pitch, stylistic acuity, and tonal beauty. Despite a heavy academic course load, she valued her time playing and singing jazz in the nonmajor combo program and singing in one of the university's co-ed a cappella groups. When asked why she did so much music in addition to her academic major, she replied, "You can't work all the time. It takes away the stress. I've found music just does that. I just can't ever imagine my life without music."

Zach

Raised in upstate New York, Zach grew up singing in children's choirs and at various church and civic functions. He was also an outstanding baseball player—so much so that he was recruited to college as the new catcher for the team. During his formative years, Zach "hung out with the superjocks" but also with those who loved to make music. His passion for music and his musical development he attributed to his mother, who "forced him" to either sing or play an instrument every year until he graduated high school. Zach chose singing in school because he "sucked at playing the drums." Even though Zach frequently made All-County Choir, was selected for solos in his auditioned high school Chamber Ensemble, and was the lead in the school musicals, Zach did not see himself as musically literate: "I can't read music. I have no idea of any music terminology besides understanding some dynamic symbols, like forte and crescendo and decrescendo. That's the extent of my musical knowledge."

Zach's chorus teacher in high school sang opera in regional opera houses. She was an important figure in his life who wanted him to become a music major. Despite his love of singing, he didn't want to "do the conservatory." After being accepted to a liberal arts college during his senior year in high school, he attended the activity fair to look for ways to continue singing. While at the activity fair, members of the all-male a cappella group on campus approached Zach and asked him to audition. Zach enjoyed his first semester with the a cappella group so much that he became interested in pursuing a minor in music. Unfortunately, the college's required choral ensembles met at the same time as baseball practice so he was not able to pursue this interest.

Zach expressed a variety of reasons for making music. "I love hanging out with a bunch of guys and getting to sing. We also hang out outside of rehearsal and party on the weekends." Though the social aspects of music were important to Zach, he believed that, similar to his sports experiences, having fun also means working hard. Zach's first-year a cappella experience turned out very well. "It's making my college experience better because I'm hanging out with more people and different people. I'm not just hanging out with baseball players; I'm hanging out with people that enjoy music."

When Zach returned home after his first year of college, he ran into his former music teacher. He told her that he was in an a cappella group. She was unimpressed. Through clenched teeth she replied, "Oh that's *great*. So how about that music minor?" When asked if he would continue baseball after college, Zach thought for a moment and said, "Naw. I know this is my last four years of baseball and I'm trying to get the most out of it that I can, because after this, it's the 'real world,' and I can't be playing baseball and working at the same time. That's just too hard. But I would love to learn an instrument or sing in a band."

The Problem

While not necessarily representative of all students who remain musically active in collegiate a cappella during their undergraduate studies, the stories of Michelle and Zach help to illuminate the determined but arbitrary pathways and experiences that sustain musical involvement beyond the secondary school years. As music educators, our interests lie not so much in the cultural aspects of a cappella *qua* a cappella (though this is an important contextual factor) as they do in how this particular musical phenomenon might inform, and what it might reflect about, lifelong music making in the broader context of people's lives. On the one hand, we are cautiously encouraged that, among the college-going population, there is, by many measures, substantial interest in volitional music making in a student-run, recreational practice like collegiate a cappella. On the other hand, there is relatively little research on how musical participation during the college years might impact on or translate into music making later in life. Moreover, there is a glaring absence of research that considers how a practice like collegiate a cappella reflects and manifests various differences in social life.

One of our motivations for wanting to study the lives of collegiate a cappella participants is the relationship that exists between school music practices and music making later in life. Thomas Regelski (2009) submits, "To the degree that what is taught in school has little or no lasting, life-long musical impact on students or society... [it loses] the economic and cultural support of society" (68). Ever the pragmatist, Regelski's argument is that "lasting musical impact" is best measured by lifelong music making, something that provides "proof" that school music has "made a difference." Regelski's basic point is difficult to ignore: if school music teaching is about more than just "appreciation" (which, as French sociologist Pierre Bourdieu has argued, is usually code for the imposition of the tastes of the powerful), we should expect to see some sort of observable difference in lifelong musical behaviors between those who participated in school music and those who did not.

Regelski's point is well-taken, but it glosses over many nuances. Lifelong music making, or better still, the *potential* for lifelong music making, is a product of complex socio-cultural forces. Many school music teachers, for example, believe they are teaching a "love of music," presumably meaning some sort of "lasting, lifelong musical impact." The most notable scholar who has examined relationships between school music instruction and musical activity later in life is British researcher Stephanie Pitts. Her books *Valuing Musical Participation* (2005) and *Chances and Choices* (2012b) are based on empirical studies that consider the potential impact that school music and other formative musical experiences have had on lifelong involvement in music for her participants. Pitts's research into the "lasting effects of music education" (2005, 121) illuminates a number of issues, such as how school music influences taste, self-identity as a musician, and how musical involvement contributes to social and personal fulfillment. With reference to authors such as Percy Scholes, Ruth Finnegan, and Lucy Green, Pitts problematizes the aims and impact of school music in the UK and the role teachers play in nurturing lifelong participation in music. In the big picture, we concur with Pitts about the central aim for music education: "that all students should leave school knowing enough about music to be able to pursue it further through independent learning and involvement in adult life" (2005, 134). This is not to discount the value of musical experiences as they occur in school or to imply that school music is merely preparatory for the "real" living that is to come. Rather, we would argue there is little reason to think that school music experiences cannot be simultaneously valuable in themselves *and* provide skills and dispositions for lifelong involvement.

Collegiate a cappella represents an opportunity to explore a number of questions related to lifelong, leisure-time involvement in music. Leading up to this study, we wondered, for example, about the veracity of oft-repeated claims (e.g., Regelski 2005, Jones 2009, Myers 2008b) that American school music programs fail to adequately develop the requisite musical agency for musical participation beyond the school years. Do school music graduates who participate in collegiate a cappella really lack the musicianship necessary for independent (or interdependent) music making? Or perhaps better stated: what does collegiate a cappella reveal about musicianship and the requirements for independent/interdependent music making? Following Pitts, we also wondered about the impact of formative experiences on the musical lives of those who participate in collegiate a cappella (see also Mantie 2013, Paparo 2013) and about the influences that might be inferred about participants' school music experiences. What might collegiate a cappella reveal about issues of participation, expertise, motivation, and power, for example?

The college/university years represent a pivotal period in the lives of people who might be regarded as "adults in the making."[1] Although some university

---

[1] See the literature on "emerging adulthood" (e.g., Arnett 2002).

students continue to live at home, the majority do not. For many, the college years are a liminal period of experimentation and exploration where people live simultaneously in the past and present while attempting to negotiate who they imagine to be in the future. Some of those we interviewed, for instance, would speak of their high school experiences using present tense, as if they hadn't really left that period of their lives behind. For so many of our informants, collegiate a cappella functioned as a form of identity continuation, filling a need to participate in a musical activity with a strong social component that would help alleviate the apprehensions associated with the unknowns of university.

Research in leisure studies and adult education has shown that, while some people take up completely new activities in their adult years, most are generally unlikely to suddenly take up activities with a high point of entry (such as music) as a form of what Robert Stebbins has classified and theorized as "serious leisure" (www.seriousleisure.net). It was this recognition that led Roy Ernst to create New Horizons International Music Association as an entry point for older adults (55+) to learn to play in large ensembles like bands, orchestras, and choirs (see newhorizonsmusic.org). It is wonderful that such opportunities exist in some communities. A concern of ours, however, has to do with the issue of *continuity*. Collegiate a cappella participants are typically volitionally involved in order to continue their music making. Unlike high school music participation in the United States, which, although usually optional, is justified by the National Association for Music Education as a core curricular subject and occurs under the auspices of learning and child-rearing, participation in collegiate a cappella is extracurricular—or in the opinion of some, co-curricular—and thus represents a form of self-selected (and student-run) leisure activity. Given that this liminal period for "adults in the making" is so crucial for their conceptualization of "lifestyle," collegiate a cappella affords an excellent opportunity to examine whether participants consider their musical involvement as a college-bounded activity or a life activity.

About the Population of Collegiate A Cappella

Since 2000, the US "immediate college enrollment rate" (i.e., those who enroll in college/university following high school graduation) has ranged between 60 and 70 percent (National Center for Educational Statistics). Given that about one out of every three people do not enroll in university upon graduating high school, studying collegiate a cappella is by no means a comprehensive way to study the issue of lifelong music making—or more precisely, in our case, issues of continuity in music making between the school years and the immediate post-schooling years. Not only does studying the college-going population overlook a large number of high school graduates (to say nothing of those who do not graduate high school), but, as our research confirmed for us, collegiate a cappella members evince a level of privilege that generally surpasses that of the general population, if not the college-going population itself. One is reminded here of the history of collegiate a cappella: this was originally, and was for a very long time, an Ivy League pursuit.

Not that one can or should infer too much from visual inspections alone, but clicking on the websites or Facebook pages of collegiate a cappella groups further reveals that participants do not appear to reflect the wider demographic of US society. A quick YouTube search for "ICCA" (International Championship of Collegiate A Cappella), for example, leaves little doubt about the whiteness of this particular music practice. This is hardly surprising. As Elpus and Abril (2011)[2] have demonstrated, students in school music programs are disproportionately white, as are their teachers (Elpus 2015).[3] From the outset of our research we have been under no illusions that collegiate a cappella is broadly (or even narrowly) "representative" of the population of the United States.

Despite its lack of racial, cultural, and socioeconomic representativeness of the population of the United States, collegiate a cappella still affords excellent opportunities to study issues of music-making continuity because it closely aligns with the demographic representativeness of a typical school music participant. Even though some (but not all) of our informants had private lesson instruction, almost all had some form of school music experience. Almost all of

---

[2] Elpus and Abril (2011) found that White students were significantly over-represented among music students, as were students from higher SES backgrounds, native English speakers, students in the highest standardized test score quartiles, children of parents holding advanced postsecondary degrees, and students with GPAs ranging from 3.01–4.0. Findings indicate that music students are not a representative subset of the population of US high school students. As Elpus and Abril state, "On every dimension we investigated that is associated with social strata and economic resources, music students tend to be significantly more privileged than their non-music counterparts" (138–9).

[3] Results from Elpus (2015) showed that music teacher licensure candidates were a highly selected subset of the population. Music teacher candidates identified as 86.02 percent White, 7.07 percent Black, 1.94 percent Hispanic, 1.79 percent Asian, 0.30 percent Native American/Alaska Native, 0.32 percent Pacific Islander, 0.82 percent Multiracial, and 1.74 percent Other. Compared to various populations of interest with known ethnic/racial compositions, people of color were significantly underrepresented among music teacher licensure candidates, while White people were significantly overrepresented. As Elpus points out, "Music teacher licensure candidates are not representative of the population of American adults, not representative of the population of currently working public school music teachers in the United States, not representative of the population of U.S. undergraduate students, and not representative of the pool of high school graduates who had persisted in music through the entirety of their high school careers" (330).

our informants referenced at least some elementary music experience (though most could not recollect much about it) and participated in high school music programs for at least one or two years. Regardless of any feelings one might have about existing inequities in school music participation (or institutionalized music teaching and learning in general), our sample is reasonably reflective of those who participated in school music programs. This does not mean that our research can or should be "generalized" to all school music graduates, or all people who involve themselves in avocational music making, but rather, that what we learned should have relevant implications for those who teach music in any capacity and/or those who care about lifelong participation in music.

As pointed out above, our informants' involvement with school music varied from heavy involvement in multiple ensembles at the high school level (including a cappella singing in a few cases) down to nothing beyond elementary school music class. It is important to be clear that, while we were (and are) interested in the "lasting impacts of music education," we do not mean to imply or suggest causal linkages through our research. Establishing causality in a strict scientific sense was never our aim (nor do we think such a thing is even possible, given the enormous number of variables one would need to identify and isolate). Rather, by studying this particular avocational music making activity, we hoped to better understand the practice and the people involved in order to raise questions about and theorize (at a basic level) issues of musical continuity during this crucially important juncture in the lives of young people.

Despite the visibility of collegiate a cappella in recent years, it should be kept in mind that, on a percentage basis, the number of participants is rather small. A large university of 30,000 students, for example, may have a dozen groups, but that still only results in 150–200 participants—barely more than 0.5 percent of the school's population. Focusing on the number of direct participants alone, however, masks the wider network of fans, organizations, and structures involved—what Christopher Small (1998) attempted to capture with the word "musicking"—that constitute the practice of collegiate a cappella. Much like how a university's sports team might galvanize the interests and activities of an entire campus, collegiate a cappella embodies, albeit on a much smaller scale than prominent campus sports like football or basketball, a similar network that exceeds the actual number of "players on the field." Collegiate a cappella alumni, which for some groups total hundreds and hundreds of people and fundraise thousands of dollars, are but one example of a node in the network that creates and sustains what has become a normalized activity on many of the nation's university campuses.

As mentioned above, collegiate a cappella is grounded in an amateur aesthetic that prides itself on its self-run nature—an aspect central to its historical identity. There are exceptions, however. The explosive growth of collegiate a cappella in the 1990s and early 2000s has led to what might be interpreted as a degree of institutionalization. On many campuses it is not unusual to require a faculty advisor for student clubs formally recognized by the university (which groups often need in order to book campus spaces), but the faculty advisor is usually a nominal role. On a small minority of campuses, however—such as in Brent's case—the advisor is a member of the university's music faculty and takes a more active role in the group, even offering rehearsal and performance advice. There are even a few campuses where students can enroll in collegiate a cappella for university credit, something that would seem to go against the grain of collegiate a cappella's co-curricular history.

About Collegiate A Cappella History

There are several sources that attempt to document collegiate a cappella's history. We've drawn primarily on two for purposes here. Duchan's (2012a) narrative approaches a cappella's history systematically and academically. In contrast, Mickey Rapkin (2008) provides something of a grand theory of the evolution of collegiate a cappella, which he suggests involves such things as the Mills Bros. in 1931, the founding of the SPEBSQSA,[4] the Dapper Dans at Disneyland in the 1950s, Pete Seeger and the Weavers singing "The Lion Sleeps Tonight," Sam Cooke with the Soul Stirrers, The Chordettes, The Nylons, Manhattan Transfer, Billy Joel, Bobby McFerrin, Paul Simon's *Graceland* album, Boyz II Men, and, most notably, the 1991 Spike Lee & Company PBS documentary, *Do It A Cappella* (Rapkin 2008, 4–5). Curiously left off of Rapkin's list (and omitted from Lee's film) are the vocal jazz groups that followed in the wake of the Mills Bros., such as the Les Double Six, Swingle Singers, Four Freshmen, and, later, the L.A. Voices, all of which, along with barbershop, gospel, doo-wop, and other vocal harmony ensembles, helped to influence the collegiate a cappella aesthetic. Arguably, however, the ensemble that provided the most important influence on today's collegiate a cappella approach was Rockapella. Originally founded in 1986 (emerging from the a cappella scene at Brown University), Rockapella rose to prominence in the public eye thanks to being the "house band" on the PBS children's show *Where in the World Is Carmen Sandiego?*, which ran from 1991 to 1995.

[4] Society for the Preservation and Encouragement of Barber Shop Quartet Singing in America.

Although collegiate a cappella can now be found across the United States (and on some college campuses beyond the United States), the largest concentration of collegiate a cappella groups is found in the US northeast. This is because historically these groups were founded in Ivy League schools, something that contributed to their original identity as an all-male pursuit. For example, the Yale "Whiffenpoofs," founded in 1909, are generally credited as being the oldest continuously operating collegiate a cappella group in the United States (Cole Porter, among the group's oldest and most famous alumni, was a member of the 1913 lineup). The modifier "collegiate" is important here, because it helps to distinguish such ensembles (then and now) as student groups, in contradistinction to those a cappella groups operating as formal institutional offerings typically led by a "qualified" choir director. Many long-standing "collegiate" groups attribute their origins to dissatisfaction with the available institutional choir. Rapkin (2008) points out, for example, that the Tufts Beelzebubs (or "Bubs") formed in the 1960s because they didn't like the chair of the music department (and he apparently didn't like the Bubs because they were raiding his choir).

Song choices, director style and/or personality, time and/or location, and all manner of other reasons may have provided the impetus for forming a student group independent from direct institutional authority. Important to keep in mind, however, is that, while these collegiate a cappella groups typically formed as part of what might be read as a form of resistance to the constraints of institutional authority (or in some cases formed as part of the glee club movement of the 1920s, 1930s, and 1940s), their repertoire and practices originally did not differ substantially from what was going on in groups led by an institution's choir director. To the best of our knowledge, the repertoire of student-run groups over the course of much of the twentieth century typically included fewer sacred and art songs but was still largely choral-based: groups sang from the same purchased octavos as their choir director-led counterparts. A member of the Massachusetts Institute of Technology Logarhythms in the 1960s, for example, reported to Roger that their repertoire generally consisted of a combination of barbershop, choral-like, and doo-wop styles.[5]

In retrospect, it is fascinating to consider how collegiate a cappella went from a niche, mostly male singing activity in elite colleges, to the widespread practice it is today. As Rapkin describes it, in the 1990s, "collegiate a cappella exploded from an

---

[5] "Old Men Singing: Documentary Short" provides a wonderful and touching window into the nature and spirit of collegiate a cappella in the mid-twentieth century. See https://vimeo.com/187474934, accessed June 1, 2020.

Ivy League curiosity to a full-blown coed pursuit" (2008, 80).[6] Fueling this growth was the founding in 1991 of CASA—the Contemporary A Cappella Society of America—an organization that helped to galvanize interest in collegiate a cappella, initially through a newsletter, but eventually a website and, most importantly, a songbook. "The biggest problem with starting a group," explained Deke Sharon, "is that they have nothing to sing" (quoted in Rapkin 2008, 177). By creating a songbook (initially of just twelve tunes) and launching an internet library, Sharon was able to generate the critical mass necessary for a wider a cappella movement to take root. Although the internet library was eventually taken down due to copyright concerns, CASA reportedly went from 250 groups to over 1250 in this early period. Duchan reports that more groups were founded in the period 1990–1999 than in the prior eighty-one years. Notable also is that by 1994, co-ed groups began to outnumber all-male and all-female groups (Duchan 2012a, 47).[7]

Commensurate with the rise of interest in collegiate a cappella in the 1990s, the repertoire and musical approach began to change. In the manner of Rockapella, groups began singing self-arranged "covers," mostly of pop music (less experienced groups sometimes purchased nonpublished arrangements through informal networks). Initially, these cover arrangements retained the homophonic choral-like textures of barbershop and choral works, but, by the 2000s, most arrangements had moved in the direction of what is typically found today: songs feature a soloist (or pair of soloists) with other members emulating the instrumental parts with vocal syllables to provide harmonic and rhythmic support. One member usually does "perc," a.k.a. beatboxing—a practice attributed to the Tufts University Beelzebubs and their 1991 album, *Foster Street*. While there are a few specialized a cappella groups on some campuses (Christian, Jewish, Korean, etc.), "mainstream" collegiate a cappella is unaffiliated. Repertoire choices are usually determined by the musical tastes and interests of the group members, balanced by pragmatic concerns about who in the group might be a suitable fit for the solo part.

It is hard not to overstate the importance of the internet on the growth of collegiate a cappella in the 1990s. The ability to share and communicate provided the missing spark needed to ignite broad-based interest. As Bill Hare, one of the major pioneering figures of "modern" a cappella, explains,

---

[6] Rapkin (2008) reports that the first female collegiate a cappella group was the Smith College Smiffenpoofs, dating to 1936. He reports the 1973 Princeton Katzenjammers as the first co-ed group.

[7] In *So You Want to Sing A Cappella: A Guide for Performers*, something of a how-to manual for those interested in a cappella singing, Deke Sharon (2018) provides a personal account of his role in the explosion of the modern-day a cappella movement.

> If it weren't for this new form of instant information gathering, most groups would have remained islands unto themselves—I know the Stanford groups for the most part didn't know there were any other groups out there before this time... I was really impressed when I got a letter from this kid Deke Sharon in Boston who had heard my work with the Mendicants from all the way over in California. (quoted in Duchan 2012a, 61)

Increased communications and awareness were catalyzed by the development of some very forward-thinking individuals like Bill Hare and Deke Sharon, who helped to create an organizational infrastructure that continues to sustain collegiate a cappella activity.

> Institutional structures such as the CAN [Collegiate A Cappella Newsletter], CASA [Contemporary A Cappella Society of America], RARB [Recorded A Cappella Review Board], BOCA [Best of College A Cappella], and ICCA [International Championship of Collegiate A Cappella] connect a cappella musicians to one another, enabling them to share in the production of an "imagined world" of collegiate a cappella and feel like active participants in a community. (Duchan 2012a, 63)

Some of the organizational infrastructure of collegiate a cappella leans toward industry. Back in the 1990s and early 2000s, for example, the collegiate a cappella recording industry became a big-money business (see Rapkin 2008). Although industry is beyond our concerns in this book, it cannot be overlooked that this aspect of the practice helps to contribute to the overall desire and interest in collegiate a cappella.

The Study

Combining our efforts, we spent over nine years (2010–2019) researching collegiate a cappella. The research sites included fourteen colleges/universities, all but two of which were in the US northeast. Six of the fourteen sites were large schools over 20,000 students. Notably, only two were "public" institutions. Three research sites were in the Top 100 in the *Times Higher Education* World Reputation Rankings (two of which are perennially in the top 10); three schools were liberal arts colleges. We observed twenty-four collegiate a cappella groups and interviewed sixty-three participants. Our interview questions included the following thematic areas:

- personal and musical histories and backgrounds;
- participants' prior knowledge of and entry point into collegiate a cappella, including their audition aspirations and experiences;

- the operational and musical functioning and aspirations of the group;
- the role and function of music in their lives;
- current musical goals, expectations, and satisfactions;
- future plans.

We approached collegiate a cappella primarily as a social practice, the study of which might provide insights into (a) connections between music learning in the formative years and later in life, (b) how participants conceptualize and enact collegiate a cappella, (c) how participants rationalize their involvement given their larger life ambitions, and (d) if and how collegiate a cappella is viewed as a form of lifelong engagement with music making.

Given that the three traditional types of collegiate a cappella groups are "all-male," "all-female," and "co-ed," we should have better anticipated that topics surrounding gender would likely emerge. Our informants often talked about being motivated to sing in one type of group over another. We quickly learned, however, that, once participants join a group, gender factors as a primary structuring component of the entire experience. Hence, although gender was not part of our original conceptualization of the research, we very quickly sensitized ourselves during interviews, allowing more space for such discussions. Predictably, perhaps, as our interview questions pursued gendered matters, sexuality emerged as another issue of importance to many of our informants.

We independently transcribed and coded our interviews and observational field notes, looking specifically for markers of musical agency, discrimination, participation, gender, sexuality, and structures of power. Over a period of six years (2014–2019) we exchanged, discussed, and wrote up our data, considering along the way the salience of various interview exchanges as they informed the constructs and arguments under investigation. Our analyses in this book draw upon different disciplines (though mainly "practice theory") to examine participation, agency, values, expertise, motivation, and power inherent in this particular social practice.

Looking Ahead

> The thing about collegiate a cappella is that it exists in this incredible space: college. It's the one time in life where everything is momentum… For the same reason one joins a fraternity, or an athletic team, one joins an a cappella group. The problem arises when you take a cappella out of the context of college—then what is it, really? A cover band. With no instruments. (Rapkin 2008, 270)

At first glance, this book could be read as a simple description of collegiate a cappella. In fact, some of our initial interests were phenomenological. For example, What is collegiate a cappella? How did it come to be? What is gained from participation in such an experience? Do participants continue engaging in this phenomenon after college? Where do participants acquire the skills to engage in this practice? Why do participants invest so much time singing when they should be studying?

Our research goes beyond mere description, however, in order to problematize and theorize the practices of music learning, teaching, and participation as they relate to what Pierre Bourdieu describes as "lifestyle." Take, for example, the cases of Michelle and Zach—real examples from our data. In their stories we can see how a tension so often exists between the altruistic goals of music educators in developing "lifelong creators, performers, and appreciators of music" and the structures of music education (training, credentialing, and certification) that too often work against bringing lifelong music-making goals to light. What does it mean, for example, to lead a "successful" *musical* life? In the case of Zach's teacher, why does participating in an a cappella group on campus not meet her goals for Zach to continue making music beyond high school? Would the credential of a music minor give him greater potential for making music beyond college? In the case of Michelle, why didn't her high school choral director see the potential she actualized in college? Where will her skills be applied after college?

Issues of lifelong music making related to school music represented a point of departure for our research, but what began as an open-ended, relatively innocent curiosity quickly expanded to include considerations of gender, sexuality, and structures of power and privilege. Although our research partially corroborates Rapkin's observation about collegiate a cappella being little more than a cover band when removed from its college context, it turns out that there is a lot more going on in collegiate a cappella than first meets the eye (and ear) when one examines what goes on beneath the covers.

2

The Locus of Enjoyment

"I like to be good, but not at the expense of happiness"

The degree pursuits of our sixty-three informants included over thirty-nine different academic majors. Regardless of arguments about the rigor or study demands of one academic program over another (or one institution over another), it stands to reason that time spent on collegiate a cappella activity is time not spent on curricular pursuits. A handful of collegiate a cappella groups rehearse as little as four hours per week, but the norm is closer to six hours—not counting extra rehearsal time preceding performances and other events. Many of our informants reported spending around ten hours per week (or more) on their a cappella activities. This seemed to us a lot of time, especially for students in our study attending institutions known for their intense degree programs. What was curious was why students would spend so much time on what one of our informants described as a "non pre-professional activity"—recalling that, with rare exceptions, collegiate a cappella singers are not music majors (e.g., our informant pool only included two music performance or music education majors).

In Chapter 1, we also documented the meteoric rise of collegiate a cappella through the 1990s and early 2000s. As previously discussed, there are some likely explanations for this rise, perhaps the most obvious being the development of the internet, which facilitated awareness and sharing—essentially creating a network and community where there had previously only been isolated instances of a cappella singing on individual campuses. What the rapid expansion of collegiate a cappella does not explain is why so many students devote so much time to what many would consider a rather niche, "subcultural" activity that has little to do with degree attainment. This curiosity led us to straightforwardly ask our informants, *Why do this?*

Due to its centrality to the collegiate a cappella world, we begin the chapter by examining the issue of competition in music, and more specifically, the ICCA's, in order to problematize the tension we gleaned from informant reports on the double-edged sword of competition—something apparently necessary for improvement, but carrying the potential cost of jeopardizing enjoyment. We then probe what participants feel they are deriving from their a cappella experience in order to problematize issues of motivation and desire. We tackle this by exploring the complex relationship between collegiate a cappella's musical and social appeal, and by interrogating the importance and limits of "being good." We also include a brief discussion of how informants conceptualize the role and function of rehearsals in relation to performances. Given that enjoyment is proximally (though loosely) tied to the ideal of "goodness," and that goodness is in many ways tied to improvement, the final data section of musical expertise and authority considers how collegiate a cappella groups grapple with maintaining the "locus of enjoyment."

A Short Music Competition Primer

Formal music ensemble competitions have existed in the United States since at least the mid-nineteenth century. Scattered records show competitions of brass instrument solo and ensemble groups, for example, convening throughout the American Midwest in the 1870s–1900s (Keene 1982). In the early 1900s, a number of music competitions for school organizations sprung up across the country, including some state contests (Williams 1996). The first "national" band contest in Chicago in 1923 generated interest and enthusiasm that helped to lay the groundwork for subsequent contests (Holz 1962). Supporters of the contest movement argued that contests provided motivation for excellence in performance as well as added incentive for participation. Neil (1944), however, reminds us that competition is a double-edged sword:

> Its strength lies in the stimulation given students to do their best; its weakness lies in the fact that it may become an end in itself. When the latter is true, the goal in the mind of the student is not that of giving a fine musical performance but rather of receiving a coveted rating. Perhaps in this idea of giving rather than receiving lies a point of departure for establishing a basic philosophy of the competition-festival itself. (158)

Despite such early expressions of concern over competition, band and singing contests went on to become a source of school pride and part of inter-school rivalries that included athletics, elocution, and music (Rohrer 2002). Music contests are today an integral part of the school music experience for American school children.

Coincident with the rise of educational music contests was the emergence of the college glee club movement and the harmonized a cappella vocalizing style now known as "barbershop."[1] It was perhaps inevitable that the belief in competition as the solution to "raising standards" that fueled the school music contest movement was mirrored in the extra/co-curricular practice of glee clubs and the recreational activity of barbershop. Winstead (2013) cites a writer for *Outlook* magazine from 1923 who took note of how the glee clubs, which used to be viewed primarily as "social" clubs, "fostered higher musical ideals" as a result of competition (167). Winstead documents a college glee club contest at Carnegie Hall in 1923, and how a thousand students from New York City's Hunter College participated in an "interclass" singing contest at the Metropolitan Opera in 1928. By 1932, the "Intercollegiate Music Council" was helping to oversee the Metropolitan Intercollegiate Glee Club Contest at Carnegie Hall.

First associated with southern black quartets singing at local barber shops in the 1870s, the barbershop style became popular in the early 1900s, as Tin Pan Alley songwriters appealed to the needs and tastes of recreational musicians, and white minstrel singers appropriated the style of the black barbershop singers with songs such as "Shine On, Harvest Moon," "Hello, Ma Baby," and "Sweet Adeline." Interest in barbershop music continued to grow in the early twentieth century, leading to the 1938 formation of the Society for the Preservation and Encouragement of Barber Shop Quartet Singing in America (now known simply as the Barbershop Harmony Society), an organization that has held annual singing competitions every year since. Notably, the organization began awarding a prize for a "collegiate quartet" category beginning in 1992.

The International Championship of Collegiate A Cappella

In 1996, the founding of the International Championship of Collegiate A Cappella[2]—or as it is referred to by participants, the "I-C-C-As"—contributed to, or perhaps responded to, the upsurge in interest in collegiate a cappella in the 1990s. At the same time, it arguably altered the nature of what collegiate

---

[1] The first written use of the word "barbershop" when referring to harmonizing came in 1910, with the publication of the song, "Play That Barbershop Chord." For a thorough overview of barbershop, see Gage Averill's (2003) book, *Four Parts, No Waiting*, which traces the popularity of this musical practice in minstrel shows, black recreational singing, vaudeville, and early recordings to its revival in the 1930s. Other notable sources include Garnet (2005), Stebbins (1996) and an edited volume by Kaplan (1993).

[2] Originally the National Championship of Collegiate A Cappella.

a cappella groups were about, moving them more in the direction of "higher musical standards." Instead of relatively simple get-togethers on campus celebrating a shared interest in singing, as a cappella had been for most of the twentieth century, the ICCAs—a series of regional competitions culminating in a final round held annually in New York City—shifted the focus of attention from recreational campus singing toward the goal of "winning."

What almost everyone in the collegiate a cappella world knows, and what we quickly learned when we began our research, is that the decision to treat singing competitively essentially defines a group's practices and identity. It was not uncommon in our interviews, for example, for people to describe their group as "competitive" or "noncompetitive." There are groups that exist for the explicit purpose of competing in the ICCAs, whereas some make a conscious decision *not* to compete in the ICCAs, and some groups make year-to-year decisions whether or not to compete in the ICCAs. One group in our study was founded as a competitive-focused group by "breakaway members" dissatisfied with existing noncompetitive options. Another group in our study was explicitly committed to being the best group in the country and succeeded in winning the ICCAs during the time of our research.

One of the things that interested us was how a group's decision to focus its efforts on the ICCAs affected its practices and how members felt about the idea of competition in music. Save for two or three informants, there were very few critical comments about the nature of the ICCA competition itself. We were surprised, for example, that more informants didn't echo Jane's observation that it was unfair for Pitch Slapped (from Berklee College of Music), a group of music majors, to participate in a competition that is fundamentally amateur in nature. We were likewise surprised not to hear more references to the judging criteria, which include a heavy emphasis on choreography. Of interest was the amount of institutional memory among group members. Phillip, for example, explained that, several years in the past, his group had only come in third at the ICCAs because they "don't do choreo" and that they have never returned to the ICCAs because they refuse to compromise their aesthetic values. It was remarkable to us how informants spoke of their group's ICCA participation from ten years prior as if they themselves had been involved with it.

We gleaned that, among groups that competed in the ICCAs on an irregular basis, there were often divided opinions among members (e.g., "I wish we were more competitive. We were going to do ICCAs this year, but it's a lot of work and some of the other girls aren't as committed"). The ambivalence over the ICCAs is understandable. Not only do groups have to pay in order to compete, which, for less financially secure groups (typically all-female), represents a significant barrier, but the intense preparation among some groups (e.g., references to ten-hour rehearsals in advance of the competition) is likely a turnoff for those members who simply "want to sing." Not surprisingly, when asked about the ICCAs, we heard comments like "we don't have time to prep for them."

Several informants mentioned that their group no longer competed in the ICCAs because the experience had been less than positive. As an informant of an all-female group explained, "We tried to be an ICCA group, but in the process we lost our way." This *losing of the way* theme percolated up in a few groups. There were several references to how some members became frustrated by the competitive aspects and the level of intensity involved with ICCA preparation (e.g., "there were unhappy times in the group because of the competition"; "we used to do ICCA's, but didn't like competing"; "we don't like the judging at ICCA's; we see singing as fun, not competitive").

The ICCAs represent only one aspect of competition in collegiate a cappella, of course. Participants typically go through a rigorous audition process to get in, for example. "I'm not aware of an all-comers a cappella group," one informant reminded us. Additionally, in many groups there are internal voting processes to determine soloists on songs, and participants are continually comparing their group with other groups. The overwhelming sentiment among our informants—perhaps reflecting larger societal values about the importance of competition—was that competition was positive if not outright essential (e.g., "you can only get so good without competition"; "it makes you hold to a higher standard"). There were several informants, however, who offered a dissenting view (e.g., "music is not the right place for competition"; "I have a disdain for competitive music"). One group took a pragmatic approach to the problem of competition, explaining, "During spring we're competitive, during fall we're not."

Some informants exhibited a good deal of thoughtfulness about the question of competition in music, often noting the "benefits and downsides." Austin remarked that competition can be both good and bad. "It is good when it raises the quality of what you've got, but bad when you don't give people the opportunity." Austin reflected on the fact that at the high school level people should have opportunities to learn and should not have these cut short in the interests of competition: "There are times you feel awful about yourself [due to competition]. In high school I didn't like that." On the flip side, he bemoaned the seeming fragility of some of his student friends who may not have had as much exposure to competition as he did: "I notice here there are people who have never been rejected in their life."

Other responses to our questions about competition seemed conflicted. Jeremiah, a member of a recently formed co-ed group, commented on how the ICCAs are "a really awesome opportunity. They provide a lot of motivation and drive to push groups farther than they've gone before. That was definitely our experience this year." He went on, however, to clarify that the competitive aspects of the ICCAs needed to be kept in perspective: "They are also a little overrated in their importance. I realized when we were in the semi-finals that my life would be the same whether we scored at the top or the bottom." In another interview with two members of a competitive all-male group, the informants seemed to want to have their cake and eat it too. They insisted that you needed the competitive event in order to have a goal to work toward ("competition makes you work hard at something to get better") but then claimed that they themselves participated for the fun of singing, not to enter competitions. Competition was "good as long as you treat it individually," but they personally preferred "being in the middle of social and competitive."

Intriguingly, the vast majority of comments about competitive group comparisons came from female informants. As Beth, who mentioned searching YouTube for comparisons, lamented, "We're always kind of competing." This sentiment often extended to a feeling that groups had to compete with themselves. After a particularly successful performance, a member of an all-female group reflected, "We were stressed out [because of the performance]. We had to outdo ourselves!"

Motivation and Desire

Formal competitive events in music date back thousands of years. The desire to "win" seems to be so deep-seated that people are motivated to focus and to sacrifice in order to achieve the reward (which in many cases is nothing more than reputation). In psychology, a reward external to the activity itself is labeled as "extrinsic motivation." (Punishment and fear can also be extrinsic motivators.) When occurring in the context of remunerated employment in music, the motivation to excel can be understood as related to job security: one needs to be "good" or one isn't hired—ergo, employment serves as extrinsic motivation. Noncompetitive recreational musical pursuits may have other extrinsic motivators (e.g., ego, opportunities for social bonding or "hooking up"), but, given the substantial time commitment of collegiate a cappella, it seems reasonable to believe that participants are influenced more by *intrinsic* than extrinsic motivations. This is likely true even among most members of competitive groups, since, in the larger context of collegiate a cappella, the percentage that move on past the regional level of the ICCAs is very small. This raises the question of what the intrinsic motivators for a cappella participation are. To get a better sense of this, one of our main questions of every participant was *Why do this? What do you get out of it?*

Rather than begin with *a priori* motivation frameworks, such as Ryan and Deci's self-determination theory or Bandura's self-efficacy theory, we approached the problem of motivation inductively. (We hesitate to label it as grounded theory, though some may choose to describe it that way.) Our only major assumption about motivation was that involvement was considered voluntary and not coerced or subconsciously manipulated. We maintained a healthy skepticism that kept considerations of a cappella as work-avoidance, procrastination, and irresponsibility on the table, but our approach to our informants' responses was not to doubt or question their sincerity, nor their judgment. With the very rare recent exception of institutions that have started to offer collegiate a cappella for credit, participants normally receive no extrinsic rewards for their involvement. Hence, they engage volitionally on the basis of perceived "intrinsic" benefits.

Locus is a Latin word that means location, place, or position. In psychology, the "locus of control" refers to a person's attributional beliefs related to success and failure: an internal locus of control describes attributing success or failure to one's own efforts and abilities, whereas an external locus of control describes attributing success or failure to factors beyond one's control, such as fate, luck, or chance. In this chapter we adapt the idea of locus in order to examine the desires and interests of collegiate a cappella participants—people whose involvement with a time-consuming "non pre-professional" activity is best explained, we feel, by *enjoyment*. We undertake our examination of enjoyment in this chapter in light of research that has considered the motivations of recreational music makers (e.g., Brown 2012, Coffman 2008, Pitts 2005, Tsugawa 2009). Our interests here are more descriptive and generative than comparative, however. In part this is because the extant research doesn't go much beyond finding that people usually participate for a mix of "musical" and "social" reasons, a conclusion that fails to add much nuance to what lay people intuit on their own. Our interview questions attempted to drill down on the question *Why do this?* in order to better flesh out the locus of enjoyment.

The majority of our informants were involved in serious programs of study and stressed that their school work took priority over their a cappella activities. Almost all, however, also acknowledged that a cappella activities provided the impetus for being organized and disciplined so that homework never disrupted their rehearsals or performances. A few of our informants admitted that they were less serious about studies. For them, a cappella was a passion that defied rational explanation:

> I hate to admit this, but I put this before school work so often. I'm not an academic. I don't like test-taking. And so the fact that this is more fun—even though it might be more work than my school work—I want to work on this more. And I want to go to rehearsal, and I want to have fun even though it's demanding and it takes up a lot of time. And in the end it doesn't even count for anything since I'm not going to graduate with any sort of musical recognition. I really don't have a good reason. I just love doing it. And I think that's why we're all so dedicated. We're all on the same level: you get your homework done at another time because you know you have rehearsal every Thursday and Sunday. (Kelly)

An intriguing point to ponder, given the intense involvement reported by so many of our informants, is whether collegiate a cappella participation represents a form of escapism. One of our questions challenged informants to declare their involvement as a healthy activity (like eating fruits and vegetables) or a guilty pleasure (like eating chocolate). With a few unapologetic exceptions from informants who stressed the importance of guilty pleasures, most considered their activity as healthy and responsible. Answers from many informants evinced an element of self-care (e.g., "you need something for pleasure," "it keeps you sane," "having a clear knowledge of what I like to do is really beneficial for me"). Two informants at one of the high-status institutions (per the *Times Higher Education* World Reputation Rankings) made clear that some sort of recreational artistic outlet was critical to counterbalance the effects of an intense academic degree focused almost exclusively on math and science. Time spent singing was described as responsible and necessary. Other informants were more pragmatic, saying things like, "You want to do something outside of classes. It gives you a reason to study and get work done." Occasionally, informants were caught off guard by these two questions. Julie, for example, reflected, "What do I get out of it? I have fun. But now I'm thinking: what *do* I get out of it?" Similarly, Terry said with a laugh, "Why do this? I have no idea!"

The Musical-Social Nexus

> Many leisure activities go together with intended or unintended sociability either as the main goal (e.g., visits), or as a byproduct of some other goal (e.g., playing a game of soccer, attending a concert). In both cases, spending time together affects people's social bonds. (Van Ingen and Van Eijck 2009)

There can be no overlooking of the very social nature of collegiate a cappella. That said, there are other social options available to university students—ones that don't involve such a heavy investment of time and energy. It would seem that, in most cases, participants were drawn to collegiate a cappella out of a love of singing. Sociability, to the extent it was anticipated, was simply an ancillary benefit. One of our interview questions asked informants if their participation was "more about themselves" or "more about the group." Some informants openly admitted that when they originally joined their group, they were motivated by self-interest in singing. Over time, however, they noted how their interests and commitment were guided increasingly by group considerations.

For many informants, social considerations were front and center. Friends were mentioned in almost every single interview. Carla remarked that there is a lot of "serious bonding" in collegiate a cappella. "We hang out a *lot*," she said. Similarly, Keri commented that "we feel like a huge family." This is not to suggest every single group was uniformly cohesive or that every group's members would be friends in the absence of the singing pretense. Alyson, for example, said that her group would "totally fail as a social group." She went on to describe the group as very friendly and harmonious but that it was more of a "structured social group." For many members, however, their collegiate a cappella group was a central component in their social existence. Emily went so far as to say, "It's not just a group. It's my life!" Indeed, even though we heard stories of occasional tensions among group members, it was repeatedly emphasized that, when given a choice between leaving and staying in the group, almost everyone chose to remain in their group.

To distinguish between the musical and the social is to impose an artificial dichotomy on group music making. Because so many informants referenced the desired and desirable social aspects of their involvement, however, we asked them to name a percentage breakdown, musical to social, that represented their reasons for participation. It is impossible to truly separate the social from the musical, of course, and yet all informants seemed to understand the question and our reason for asking it. Some struggled to answer, perhaps intuitively grasping the specious dichotomy that was being imposed. The majority of responses fell within a 40/60 to 60/40 split, although there were a few informants that went as high as 20/80 or 80/20. Many of the more experienced informants (i.e., those in their third or fourth years in a group) mentioned how their percentage changed over time. They admitted that originally their musical interests and motivations outweighed the social but that over time these balanced out or swung in the direction of social over musical.

Being Good and the Limits of Commitment

What was abundantly clear from our observations was that groups weren't just "hanging out" socially; they were unmistakably serious about their music. Zach (from Chapter 1), described the seriousness of the recreational activity this way:

> I'm going to make an analogy: I like playing baseball because it's fun. That doesn't mean that we go and goof around for two hours, call it a day, and don't win any games. It's fun because you're putting in hard work. In music, you go and perform for an elderly center and you see them smile and it's like you just put in half a semester's work perfecting songs and we sound great and you're making people happy. They come up to you after and they're like, "you guys did a great job." And that's the fun part, I think. Putting in the hard work is important.

Like several others we interviewed, Zach repeatedly emphasized the importance of hard work. Presumably, however, there are limits to the amount of hard work participants are willing to commit in pursuit of musical and performance standards in their recreational activities.

Our informants cared very much about "being good." Wilson stressed the importance of this, saying, "You want to be part of a group that's good!" It is easy to say you want to be good, of course, but what, precisely, are a cappella participants prepared to sacrifice in the name of goodness? We would ask, "You say that being good is important, but if you really want to be good, and six hours of rehearsal gets you 'X' good, why not rehearse ten hours in order to be better?" When informants would rationalize that five to six hours was the ideal amount of time (which most always did), we would respond with: "Why not sing easier arrangements so you can polish them more? Or do fewer pieces each term so you can spend more time on each one?" Their responses to this line of questioning demonstrated that the question of *How good is good enough?* is far from straightforward.

The locus of enjoyment for our informants was not found within musical performance standards alone but reflected an intricate calculation of "costs" that involved the social aspects of group singing. Many informants acknowledged that commitment levels and aspirations of individual members varied within their group. "I'm happy doing four bars over and over, but not everyone else is," Gary explained. Similarly, Emily noted the importance of "balancing the dynamics—as with any team." A few of the more experienced informants noted that, even within their own groups, priorities changed from year to year as a reflection of changing membership. Commenting on the four years with his group, for example, Barry observed that it "has gotten tight at the expense of talent."

Some of our informants wished their groups would strive to raise their performing level but most understood the cost-benefit nature of musical improvement. Derek summed up his approach to rehearsing this way:

> Better to move on to the next song or cap rehearsal in order to—for productivity—in terms of, you know ... As an economics major, I'm thinking in terms of marginal returns. At a certain point the curve is going to get diminishing returns. At a certain point, you add an extra hour and you only get one percent better as opposed to the first hour of rehearsal you're going to get forty percent better.

References to diminishing or marginal returns came up several times in our interviews. Patrick, for example, lamented the reality of the effort required for polished improvements in response to our question about adding rehearsal time in order to get better: "The amount that it would take to get from as good as we are to excellent is not another four hours a week; it's another ten hours a week—if not more. And that's not worth it to me." Patrick's assessment more or less captures the sentiments of the majority of our informants, who expressed the desire to be good, but not at any cost.

One of the key takeaways from our data is the difference between understanding "good" as being *as good as possible* versus good as being beyond a particular threshold. A seemingly benign observation, this would seem to be a critical and overlooked understanding in music teaching and learning fields, where "excellence" (as good as possible) is typically a central operating principle. That is, institutionalized music teaching is, almost without exception, predicated upon the belief that what matters most is *excellence*—inevitably defined according to being better than almost everyone else (i.e., "the best"). In the professional world nothing is ever "good enough," because excellence is an infinity concept. One can always be better. For many of our informants, however, what mattered wasn't "excellence" but the satisfaction of being good. For them, the locus of enjoyment was found in the participation itself. One strived to be good, especially when competing in the ICCAs, but as a rule, good was defined in relation to a self-defined benchmark, not normative comparisons.

> So I'll say I think it's very important to be good enough—to be above a certain threshold of quality. Beyond that, I don't really care. I think we're good enough. We're above this minimum threshold. If we were much, much worse—I mean, below a certain level—I would not want to participate. But getting above that threshold? To go from good to extremely good? I don't really care. (Patrick)

As evident in the response above, musical standards are a subjective matter. Sustained involvement with recreational music making is typically determined by a threshold of acceptability relative to each individual's expectations. Drop below this threshold and the costs of participation outweigh the enjoyment rewards. These enjoyment rewards, however, do not directly correspond with perfection-based trajectories of excellence, whereby enjoyment is commensurate with performing level. For most collegiate a cappella singers, in other words, the locus of enjoyment does not reside within a perfectionist paradigm. As Emily put it, "I just want things to sound good," by which she didn't mean perfect, but *good enough*. Or, as pointedly summed up by Richard, "I like to be good, but not at the expense of happiness," a comment that makes clear that, for recreational music makers, participation is about more than just musical excellence.

Rehearsing and Performing

In order to dig deeper into the nature of collegiate a cappella, one of our interview questions asked about the importance of performance to the overall experience (e.g., *Is this more about the singing or the performing for you?*). A few informants were adamant about the importance of performance. Jenny, for example, responded, "Performances are so fun. You get to be a new person. You get to be on stage, and—I know for me I would in a heartbeat be a performer. That would be so fun for my life." Others, however, were a bit more suspect about what they perceived as the naiveté of some collegiate a cappella participants.

> I think people who get into college a cappella groups are the same people who wait in the parking lot for five days to sing on *American Idol*. These are people who—whether it's a real career aspiration or just a fantasy—just want to get up and perform in front of people. I like performing in front of people, but I am just as happy if not happier practicing with the group. It's about the sound and it's about the fun and it's about the guys. It's fun to entertain people, I guess, but I'm just as happy if not happier entertaining myself. (Ron)

Two informants reinforced this idea, reflecting on how the locus of enjoyment was to be found more in the rehearsals than on the performance stage. Anika said, "Obviously we love sharing our music with audiences, but I think I might be okay if we just sang with each other. I would be fine with that." Similarly, Valerie emphasized how, when placed in context, rehearsals weren't just preparation for the "real thing"; they were the real thing: "I think about how the majority of our experience in a cappella is in rehearsal, and it's like—we spend more time rehearsing than we do performing, obviously. I feel like I would still be okay with not performing. I have fun at rehearsals."

Responses such as Ron's, Anika's, and Valerie's, while not necessarily reflective of the majority, who still, for the most part, viewed the goal of performance as central to their drive to improve, serve as a reminder of the complicated relationship between motivation and enjoyment. For some participants, rehearsals are a means to an end, whereas others recognize rehearsals as a potential end in themselves. The extent to which rehearsals were viewed as a "necessary evil" rather than part of a holistic process likely also varied among participants. Although only speculative on our part, it is interesting to consider the role the informants' school music experience, which in the main reflects a means-to-an-end approach to rehearsing, may have played in conditioning their feelings about locus of enjoyment.

Musical Expertise and Authority

Competence is endemic to all performance-related practices. This is to suggest that intentionality and aspiration lie at the heart of performative practices (see Chapter 6), and that feelings of success and enjoyment are, almost without exception, determined by meeting (or surpassing) one's goals. One attempts, in other words, to do something well. Given that performance practices are cultural (rather than naturally occurring), an obvious problem is how people generate particular performance goals and how they develop the necessary competence in order to meet these goals, especially given the well-documented linear correspondence between goals/competence and motivation. How, in other words, does one develop the competence necessary to participate in collegiate a cappella?

Almost all of our informants participated in school music programs—ones that reflected the norm of choirs, orchestras, and bands. These ensembles sometimes attain performance levels that rival that of some university groups. The *individual* musicianship of members in school ensembles, however, is typically far below that of the collective musicianship. No matter how talented the individual, a generalized school music experience cannot compare to specialized training of a university degree, a claim made clear when one of the music directors in our study, in response to our prompt suggesting that their group could be better if they did half as many songs, said, "I don't think we could do four songs [rather than eight] any better." Or as another admitted, "We've had three years of exponential growth in how good we sound, but now we've hit a plateau," indicative of the limits of expertise that typically exist in the collegiate a cappella world.

The norm in collegiate a cappella today is for groups to create their own arrangements of "contemporary hits." Arranging—especially that of "covering" pop tunes with voices alone—requires knowledge of form, harmony, rhythm, and so on. Although digital audio technology and the internet have helped make easier what thirty years ago was exceptionally difficult (an intriguing causal explanation for the explosion of a cappella activity in the past thirty years or so), musical arrangements nevertheless still require a base level of knowledge that typically exceeds what a high school music graduate is likely to attain.

Having an arrangement on paper (or as a MIDI file) is only a prerequisite for attaining performance goals. Because arrangements typically involve anywhere from four to eight parts—many of which require "part independence"—and most individual singers are not able to sight-sing their parts, some form of musical leadership is required in order to rehearse the group. The music director (MD) is a member of the group voted into the position by the membership. In our observations, the musical level of each group was determined not only by the musicianship of the members but by the musical and leadership abilities of the MD. Given the typically authoritative nature of large ensemble leadership ("conductors") that students experience in school music programs, we were curious about the process of how the MD was elected and of the relationship this person had to the peers in the ensembles.

Groups in our study appeared to adopt a very pragmatic stance when it came to electing their MD. When asked directly how a group decides on their MD, most informants said they chose the person perceived to have the greatest musical competence, which, in most cases, was considered self-evident within groups. Emily, the MD of an all-female group, was forthright, saying, "If there was someone else who knew more [than me] I would have voted for them." Craig, a member of a co-ed group, put it in even starker terms, drawing attention to how musical competence ultimately trumps other considerations, such as personality.

> Even though I ran for Music Director, I ended up voting for Andrew because he's also an arranger. And I arrange songs, but his are much better than mine. I just think that he has a better grasp on music than I do. So I feel I definitely vote in terms of how well they understand music theory and leading a group. Not necessarily even their charisma in terms of leading the group—just, like, their understanding. (Craig)

Craig's reference above to music theory and a "grasp on music" are telling. Gary, the MD of a co-ed group, went out of his way to explain how a cappella groups are made up of "singers" and "musicians." Those who come from a choral background "can't see the forest for the trees," he stated. He was adamant that, when it came to leading a group, "people who are musicians get better results than singers."

Members all seemed to grasp the direct connection between the competence of the MD and the performance quality of the group. Even though the MD position is voted on (with one group in our research voting on the MD every semester), most groups seemed to be aware of the importance of a succession plan, making sure that future MDs, if not being groomed explicitly, were at least potentially waiting in the wings. In a few cases, however, planning did not seem to be as carefully thought through. As Jessica noted, "I worry about who's going to lead the group next. Musically that makes a big difference."

We witnessed a wide variety of approaches to rehearsing. Some MDs appeared to emulate the practices of their high school choir directors; others seemed to fall into some kind of routinized practices, emulating MDs of previous years. Even though groups invariably had a few members who did not read staff notation, most groups used sheet music for arrangements (sometimes read off of digital devices rather than paper), if only in the beginning stages of working on a particular piece. With a few groups, the printed notation was reified, much in the manner it so often is in school music instruction (where conductors are supposed to realize the "composer's intent"). MDs in these groups would draw attention to dynamic markings in the "score," for example, or point out how the group was singing a half note rather than the printed dotted half note. In other groups, the printed version was more of a guide, with members attending more to the performance of the sound in relation to an envisioned ideal (i.e., the recording by the original artist). One group did not use printed notation at all, and the MD taught every song by rote. While painfully slow to observe, this patient approach did appear to result in a more holistic understanding of the music among group members.

As music educators, we were interested in what MDs would attend to in rehearsals and how they would approach the task of leading the group toward an intended performance standard. In most cases (though not all), the nature of rehearsing resembled what one might typically find in a high school choir room. Admittedly, however, the observations (in Roger's case) were one-off events, thereby precluding many contextual factors that could help inform a more nuanced interpretation of the rehearsals. Still, Roger was fascinated by many of the moment-to-moment rehearsal choices. Sometimes these seemed appropriate to the goal of improving the overall quality of the performance, but there were also many instances where rehearsal choices didn't square with what he thought prudent to the situation. In some groups this appeared to be due to the limitations of the MD to hear pitch problems or rhythm inaccuracies, but in other groups where the MD appeared to possess great ears to hear issues with pitch or rhythm, the interventions seemed neither efficient nor effective (even though many resembled high school rehearsal practices). It should be added that Roger was sensitive to the possibility that what was being sought by some groups was more of an overall "effect," such as energy, emotion, or entertainment (in a good sense) rather than things such as accurate pitch locking or precise rhythmic alignment. Nevertheless, there were clear differences in musical and leadership abilities amongst the groups observed.

Effective rehearsing requires sufficient expertise in order to (a) hear the gap between an imagined ideal and what is being performed and (b) the ability to narrow the difference by causing improvement—that is, a narrowing of the gap between the ideal and the group's performance by changing the way group members are performing. A necessary part of this process involves identifying and naming "deficiency." In a school setting, the teacher-student relationship, by nature asymmetrical, not only authorizes the teacher to identify and address deficiency but in fact demands the teacher do so. This is not to suggest that all school music teachers are draconian in approach, but rather, that striving for improvement is an expectation of the job, and as such, teachers have the latitude to "call out" deficiencies. In collegiate a cappella settings, however, the MD–group relationship is rooted in reciprocity and mutual respect. Groups still wish to improve, of course, but the way in which this is achieved must be handled with sensitivity. A group can remove an MD for failing to recognize and uphold the primary directive, which is "excellence, but not at the expense of happiness" and not "excellence at all costs." This was evident in many interviews, such as in this exchange with Mallory:

> As many times as the music director is, like, I don't know, "tall vowels" or things like that—it's not that they respect them less, but it's less of a high-stakes environment. 'Cause you're, like, "I'm singing with my friends." I also think because it's peer-to-peer that the music director can only be so authoritative. Because if you're going to have a music director that's going to yell at everyone and single you out, like, "Mallory, your vowels suck," then it's not going to be fun.

Groups we observed appeared to operate on a continuum from bottom-up to top-down approaches to rehearsals. Some MDs were quite authoritative leaders of rehearsals, whereas others approached the role more as a facilitator.

From time to time, however, there were tensions in groups where roles and expectations were unclear. Zach voiced his frustration at both the inefficiency and inconsistencies in his group's approach to leadership:

> [T]he democratic part is good, but at the same time it's not productive because you'll have 30 minutes of practice where people are just talking to each other. "We should do this song. No, we should do this song. No, we should do this here. No, we need to start clapping." It's fun because you have a little bit more leeway. There's not a teacher down your throat saying, "No, you can't talk at all this rehearsal."

Among our informants were fourteen music directors. A few of them seemed quite comfortable adopting an authoritative role, saying things like, "I am not their friend during rehearsals; pissing them off yields the best results." Most, however, recognized the challenge of maintaining social aspects while still pushing the group to become better (e.g., "I had a hard time balancing being their friend versus running the rehearsal"). In Jeremiah's case, it was clear that the pursuit of being good could never take priority over maintaining the overall sense of social enjoyment:

> As one of the group's co-directors, I think a lot about the type of environment and the culture we are fostering in our group. From day one I never wanted to sacrifice the feelings of fun that we got from the group. It's valuable to get a lot of fulfillment from being good, to create good music and feel good about what you do, but ultimately if being good—if that pressure made the group not fun, if there was ever a conflict—I would always choose having fun and making people feel valued.

Paul similarly stressed "the value of promoting social aspects" in rehearsal. For him, musical improvement could never come at the expense of group happiness: "Being super strict about music is not worth it to me." He went on, however, to explain how it was still possible to achieve musical results, distinguishing between a negative approach of "calling them out" versus a positive approach of "getting them to step up." Indeed, several MDs emphasized that it was possible to walk the fine line between striving for "perfection" and "wanting to be better." As long as the right motivation was in place, said Barry, "it gives me the liberty to push them."

Although there are undeniably examples of school music teachers who abuse their authority as conductors (abuse often being rationalized as "passion" and "excellence"), most school music teachers cannot get away with excessive abusiveness simply because music at the secondary level is almost always an elective subject. Students have to want to be there, at least insofar as the perceived positives outweigh the perceived negatives. Nevertheless, the discourse of conducting pedagogy emphasizes "strong leadership." The conductor, not the students, is supposed to "know the score" and "lead" students toward an ideal performance. Even many adults in community ensembles desire a "strong leader" (Mantie and Tan 2019, O'Toole 2000). We witnessed a fair bit of "strong leadership" behaviors among the MDs we observed, but we also noted that in most groups there was a greater collective investment in the musical outcome (cf. Berglin 2015). In almost every rehearsal we observed, we noted members speaking up and offering musical suggestions during rehearsals. As Nate explained, most members tend to find their level of comfort, knowing that the group more or less operated democratically.

> It's kind of all consensus based. If there's a song you want to do or a performance where you want to talk about it, we just bring it up and say, "What does everybody think?" I think there are definitely certain members that do more in both trying to figure things out or bring things up or make things happen. And then there are some others that prefer to go along with whatever the group likes. And I think that's a good balance, actually. I think it works really well.

Conclusion: Locus or Loci?

By virtue of their participation in a volitional recreational activity, one concludes that collegiate a cappella members enjoy what they do. One also concludes that members are, almost without exception, intrinsically motivated. External motivators, such as recognition or reputation, seem inadequate explanations for why busy university students are so committed to spending so much time in "non pre-professional activity." Many students include collegiate a cappella participation on their résumés (see Chapter 5), but most institutions do not formally recognize recreational activities on transcripts. Even if or when formally recognized, there are much easier ways than collegiate a cappella for students who simply want to build their résumés. The glory of winning the ICCAs also seems unlikely as a primary motivation—particularly at the entry point. While the ICCAs may provide a motivation for improvement in many groups ("you can only get so good without competition"), nothing in our research suggests that students involve themselves in a cappella for the expressed purpose of competing.

The desire to be "good" was a consistent theme that emerged in our interviews. When push came to shove, however, it became clear that the locus of enjoyment for most informants did not reside in being flawless or in being the best but in putting forth effort and being *good enough*. While all groups strived to be their very best, mitigating considerations could temper understandings of what "very best" might mean. In one group, for example, there was a policy that each member would get a solo by junior year, a practice that suggests the pursuit of group perfectionism can be overridden by other considerations, such as the validation of each member's participation.

Our research cannot produce a strict formula for the locus of enjoyment, but it would appear there is a calculated approach operating in the form of an inverted U-shape, where enjoyment tends to increase commensurate with performance quality until the point where effort requirements overwhelm the expectations for a recreational experience (i.e., "I like to be good, but not at the expense of happiness"). The "tipping point" varied from group to group (and from member to member within a group). Understanding how far to push participants in the pursuit of excellence was a major concern among the MDs we interviewed. They understood that they were entrusted with the responsibility for ensuring an enjoyable experience: fail to achieve a desired level of "goodness" and members would be unhappy. MDs were constrained, however, by the limitations of the singers, their own musical and pedagogical limitations, and the lack of authority to "demand" improvement.

One of the questions we asked in a line of questioning related to musical standards was "How bad would the group have to be before you felt it wasn't worth your time?" This question resulted in a variety of responses, but a common theme was that members felt they would not allow their group to drop to that level. If people felt an erosion in musical enjoyment, they would not quit or stand idly by. They would intervene and implement corrective measures. In other words, while groups elect and put their faith in their MD, they still feel a sense of ownership over not just the group itself but their own personal recreational enjoyment.

That so many informants were close to a 50/50 split in their declarations of musical and social motivations is telling. Collegiate a cappella members love singing, but as importantly, they like singing with other people—especially other people with whom they feel socially connected. When the drive to improve the musical performance standard disturbs group harmony and cohesion, it undermines the group's *raison d'être*. As Roger's exchange with two members of an all-female group illustrates, the failure to reach a particular performance standard can be disappointing, but not devastating as long as the true locus of enjoyment is not forgotten. Maintaining positive relationships must always take priority overachieving musical results.

Chelsey: I think there are times when we're not good, and we're still okay with it sometimes.
Beth: Yeah.
Chelsey: Not that we're not good, but we—we don't perform as well as we could have, and we'll be disappointed about it and—
Beth: For about 20 minutes!
Chelsey: —we're like, "oh, it's not a good time to be a [group name] right now." And then we just kind of move on.
Beth: Yeah.
Chelsey: It's not the hugest blow—to an extent—within reason.
Beth: I mean, we want to make sure that it's also fun.
Chelsey: Right.
Beth: Because a lot of the time when you focus on, "Be good. Make sure you're getting those notes right"—it gets very taxing. And people are unhappy, and it's not fun anymore, and you sound worse because everyone's unhappy.
Chelsey: Well, if we were a professional company or something like that, then we wouldn't have to be friends.
Beth: Exactly.
Chelsey: Which is not what we want. Because if you're in a professional company, that's just work. Like, if you work in an office you don't have to be friends with everyone you work with. When it's school—
Beth: We're choosing to be here!
Chelsey: —Yeah!

Chelsey and Beth's comments are instructive. In a professional setting, "work" comes before socialization. Although some informants admitted they took a cappella too seriously relative to the rest of their life (meaning in relation to studying), most pointed out that, in the big picture, academics come first. Because collegiate a cappella singers are not, with rare exceptions, music majors, musical standards take a backseat to maintaining a positive and welcoming atmosphere—something well understood by most informants. "If I was a music major then it would be different," Bruce reminded us. This is not to suggest, however, that musical standards are unimportant. A recurring theme among our informants was that the social aspects were necessary but insufficient. As Jenny emphatically put it, "I wouldn't devote this much time if it was just a social activity."

There is, then, an ongoing tension that exists in recreational groups between wanting to improve musical standards—an act that, by definition, involves implicit or explicit critique of fellow group members—and not wanting to create interpersonal friction in the process. As Valerie, the assistant music director of a co-ed group lamented, "It's so tough, because that's the main thing we're struggling to grapple with right now is how to strike that balance." The role of competition exposes the importance of being mindful about the balance in efforts aimed at musical improvement. It could be said that our informants' collegiate a cappella experience fostered in many a greater sensitivity to the importance of this balance. Reports of informants feeling they "lost their way" in pursuit of ICCA success, for example, suggests a reflexivity about the locus of enjoyment.

We sensed less reflexivity related to issues of rehearsal and performance and the potential role their school music experiences may have had in conditioning their expectations and approaches, such as a means-ends approach to rehearsing and performing. Although rehearsals appeared to be carefully and systematically planned, we did not perceive much reflexivity about how rehearsal practices might vary from group to group or about how a group's understandings of specific rehearsal practices, such as the reification of printed notation, may have been influenced by prior experiences, especially those from participants' school music experiences. This is understandable, of course, in that specific learning, teaching, and facilitation practices are likely of greater interest to music educators and music teacher educators than to a cappella members.

If there is a takeaway to be had in terms of enjoyment, it may be (1) a recognition of diverse desires and expectations that exist among people who engage in recreational music pursuits such as collegiate a cappella, and (2) a deeper consideration of the ways in which desires and expectations are conditioned through socialization. That it may be more accurate and fruitful to think in terms of *loci* rather than *the* locus of enjoyment reflects, in part, human variability. It also reflects, however, the political nature of values and interests as they are advanced through processes of social interaction and social reproduction, especially schooling. Our informants' varied thoughts and opinions on competition, the importance of being good, how the pursuit of being good potentially affects group social harmony, and the role and processes of rehearsals in relation to performance all point to the complex and shifting social dynamics at play when considering enjoyment in avocational musical activity.

3

Gender and Sexuality in Collegiate A Cappella

"A cappella goggles"

> *The girls' group sang with an all-male group at the male group's school, and after they had finished the male group was like, "Wow, you sound almost as good as the guys' group"... The automatic assumption when you go on to the stage as an all-female group is that you are going to sound shrill, your set's not going to sound interesting—it's like a tie-in to* Pitch Perfect, *where he's like, "What boring estrogen set do you have prepared for us today?" That's what people expect when you come onto the stage.* (Leslie, all-female group)

Our interviewees differed considerably in their pre-college knowledge of collegiate a cappella. Some had been a cappella junkies in high school. They could name their favorite groups and were well aware of the collegiate a cappella options available at the colleges to which they applied. Others learned about collegiate a cappella during orientations and student club fares. Even among those with some prior a cappella knowledge, there were those who expressed surprise at what they learned upon entering college (e.g., "I didn't know about co-ed a cappella").

What almost everyone knows or quickly learns is that there are widely acknowledged hierarchies in the collegiate a cappella world, where all-male groups are considered the most talented, all-female groups are considered the least talented, and co-ed groups land somewhere in between. These hierarchies reflect and sustain issues of gender and sexual privilege—something too often overlooked in the gloss of happy-go-lucky college singers (or books that promote a cappella singing as always and automatically good). This is not to suggest anything nefarious or evil. Almost every person we interviewed loved being in their a cappella group, and, based on our research, we remain convinced about the value and potential of collegiate a cappella singing as a healthy and rewarding leisure-time activity. That said, it would be naïve to duck one's head in the sand and pretend that singing is just about singing. Music making is always about more than the music.

Status and Hierarchies

Due to the auditioning practices at most institutions, status reputations serve to sustain existing hierarchies. The best male singers want to end up in the all-male group(s); the best female singers do *not* want to end up in the all-female group(s). Sandra, the music director (hereafter: "MD") of an all-female group, recognized this point: "Reputation matters when auditions come around because it determines who you get. About half our group couldn't read music when I started. Clearly we weren't getting our pick of girls." As a result of auditioning practices, the most sought-after male singers tend to end up in all-male groups and the most sought-after female singers tend to end up in co-ed groups. Our all-male group member informants were quick to point out, for example, how "guys in co-ed groups are ones we turned down" or how co-ed males were "the rejects" from their group. A parallel situation exists for females, where the all-female groups "get the leftovers." When asked what kind of group they wanted to be in, almost every single female interviewee responded, "Definitely not all-female!" Interestingly, this was even the case at an all-female college, where a co-ed group existed due to a long-standing partnership with another university (that used to be all-male). As one of the informants from the group described, "as a co-ed [member] you stand out here; the other [all-female] groups feel threatened."

The status hierarchy of collegiate a cappella exists within an institution and across institutions. In our research we found only one university, notably one that is geographically removed from the college density of the American northeast, where an all-female group was considered the top ensemble on campus. This particular group was well-respected by its peers, but interviews uncovered a general perception that it had attained its status because it was for many years the only group on campus and that, with time, the co-ed groups would eventually catch up if not overtake it in quality. In one of our cases, a co-ed group was recognized as the top group at its university. Outside of these two instances, however, perceptions and opinions were otherwise consistent that all-male groups were at the top of the a cappella status hierarchy.

Reasons for the desirability of all-male or co-ed groups varied. Our informants' opinions on vocal range are interesting for what they reveal about how members rationalized their own preferences and participation in collegiate a cappella, and for what they reveal about perceptions (or perhaps more accurately at times, misperceptions) about the voice in the context of group singing. Male members of co-ed and all-male groups, for example, consistently referred to how men blended better or how co-ed groups afforded greater musical options or benefits (e.g., "The human ear has full range. All-female isn't as satisfying; you need males"). Many females agreed with the necessity of having male voices. One co-ed female member drew attention to successful all-female groups like Delilah and Noteworthy, but ultimately she concluded, "All-female a cappella just isn't that good. It just isn't that exciting… [F]emale just lacks bass." Another female co-ed member remarked that co-ed groups provided the best sonority: "I think the co-ed is far more interesting than [single sex]… The range of sound is just so much more interesting. It [all-female] just doesn't compare."

Members of all-female groups consistently acknowledged the perceived deficiencies of groups without males. Some saw this as an accepted sonic limitation: "guys groups can do more"; "we're missing the bottom, so it sounds incomplete"; "It's hard to achieve a full sound. We'll never be as loud." While classical voice pedagogues may be disturbed by what might be interpreted as a harmful vocal practice (what Allsup (2016, 39) poetically calls "the canard of protecting and promoting the healthy voice"), a few members of all-female groups noted how the desire for lower vocal sounds helped to increase their vocal range and how singing in an all-female group led to the revelation that some females are capable of singing much lower than is often thought (see O'Toole 2000). As Emily bragged about her group: "We like to call ourselves the female group with balls." In a couple cases, members of all-female groups drew attention to the importance of the musical arrangement (e.g., "by nature we're going to have to arrange differently"), although a subtext to this was the perceived inferiority of the all-female sound: "with a good arrangement it doesn't have to sound like all-female."

The perceived need for lower vocal sounds was recognized by some female informants as a factor contributing to male privilege. One all-female informant, for example, observed how the desire for a fuller vocal range contributed to the status hierarchies: "I can see why females go for co-ed. They go for the best sound." Or as another co-ed female sheepishly acknowledged, "I admit it: when a guy is in a group it just sounds better." An all-female member tried to rationalize the desire for males in another way. She accepted that males make things sound better, but at a cost: "it makes it more complicated" (in reference to social interactions).

The social dynamics within collegiate a cappella (discussed below) indeed complicate understandings of status hierarchies. Justin's comments, for example, highlight how vocal preferences become intertwined with social considerations. About his experience of being in and preferring an all-male group, he said:

> I get to say more things that come to my mind. I get to be myself around everybody, and I am myself around everybody, but there are things that you have to hold back, that you want to say but aren't necessarily appropriate in front of girls. But that's not the main reason I wanted to do just guys. I honestly think that an all-male singing group sounds the best out of all the voice parts singing together… There's great quality to women's voices, and I love it, as well as men's and women's voices. I don't know how to describe it. I like the sound of a bunch of guys singing.

Collegiate a cappella members' evaluations of other groups demonstrate that participants are acutely aware of the hierarchies that exist within and beyond their college campus. Their views on hierarchies also expose status awareness and priorities in the collegiate a cappella world. As Sandra explained:

> There is friendly competition between the three all-female groups on campus. We are constantly ranking ourselves against other groups. Others probably wouldn't agree, but I believe we are the best female group on campus. We have the best arrangements and the best basses. They even warm up with the boys! We also have the best blend. Our soloists aren't as strong. Our perc [i.e., beatboxing] is comparable, but not quite up to co-ed, though.

Two male a cappella members from one of the world's top-ranked universities put the question of status and evaluation more coyly: "It depends on how you define your hierarchies. There are a number of variables. I won't say we're the top group. We have won events and are a featured group, but every group is special." The variables referenced by these two informants are interesting to ponder. The connections between status and performance abilities are extremely complex, something fueled in part by the competitive aspects of the collegiate a cappella world and the evaluative capabilities of the often-competent but untrained participants, who would occasionally say things like "the other a cappella groups we hear, they go flat" or "their reputation is bigger than their talent."

While it rarely approached the level of sour grapes, it was interesting to us how participants in the lower-status pools (i.e., co-ed group males and all-female group females) subsequently rationalized their current involvement (e.g., "This was not my first choice but I'm so grateful here" "this is where I ended up and stuck with it"; "I originally wanted co-ed, but now I like this so much").

It is important to note, however, that very, very rarely do collegiate a cappella members ever get to experience more than one form of participation during their college years. Ergo, comparisons are imaginary and vicarious.

Single-Sex Dynamics

- *Low ceiling room; very hot (the day was very warm); everyone is looking very sweaty.*
- *They are on a 5-minute break; several are eating (supper); everyone is socializing.*
- *[At] 8:25 they get back to work; they gather around the ping-pong table in the center of the room (looking inwards at each other). They clearly like to sing; there are no inhibitions; they sing and move freely, not worried about how they look (despite me being in the room).*
- *As with [all-female group at a different university], at the end of the song there is general discussion (everyone participates); such a collective sense of trying to improve!*

(Field notes: all-female group rehearsal, March 21, 2012)

* * *

- *As with the male rehearsal I observed the other day, many here are without shoes/boots on.*
- *This group sounds really, really good. Interesting how "social" the group is. During breaks in the action there are little comments; lots of laughter. It's hard to imagine not having fun in this group. (An interruption having to do with waxing eyebrows.)*
- *"Girls let's get up and sing." They really said "girls"! (cf. other all-female groups always referred to members as "guys.")*

(Field notes: all-female group rehearsal, April 5, 2012)

Several informants discussed the close camaraderie that existed within their group and how important it was in helping to establish friends during their freshman year at college (e.g., "All of sudden there are 12–15 girls who are your best friends and that's really nice to have"). This was perhaps unsurprising, given the sheer number of hours that groups spend together. In the cases of the all-male and all-female groups, there were often references to sororities and fraternities, although occasionally this was in a sense of contrast rather than comparison. Rhonda, for example, in reflecting back on her first semester when she was deciding whether or not to accept an offer into an all-female group, remarked, "At first I thought, 'Oh no, this is going to be like a sorority and I don't want that.' But it's better than that because you're actually *doing* something together."

A few informants expressed feelings of discomfort being in single-sex environments prior to their involvement with collegiate a cappella (e.g., "I don't do well in all-male or all-female atmospheres"). An informant from an all-female college shared that she was frequently asked by friends and family—males and females alike—"How can you stand to be around so many women?" Indeed, two of our informants spoke explicitly about their initial concerns. Julie, the music director of an all-female group, shared that she "traditionally doesn't hang out with girls" and that she "socially [doesn't] like large groups of girls." Upon acceptance into the group following the auditioning period in her freshman year, her group held a scavenger hunt as a bonding experience, something that only served to reinforce Julie's doubts about joining an all-female group. Ultimately, however, she reported being happy to have found female companionship through her collegiate a cappella experience ("it gets goofy and I really like the girls in the group"), though she added that there are times where she had to "take a step" back from the intensity of so many females together.

Sandra was even more forthright in expressing her reticence about all-female environments. Having always "gotten along better with guys," she was "terrified about getting into an all-girl group." Like Julie, she was grateful to have found female companionship through her collegiate a cappella experience. She relayed how her group "taught me about how to hang out with girls." She was relieved that she received sympathy when insisting that the group not rehearse during the Super Bowl game, for example. In her words, she met "the first girlfriend I could bro out with." Due to her historical aversion to being around girls, her election as the group's music director was unexpected. "I'm floored that they allow me to be a leader." She went on to say, "I love every second I spend with them; they're my friends and my family." Keeping it real, however, she added: "That doesn't mean I don't hit points when I'm girled out."

For both Julie and Sandra, their single-sex collegiate a cappella group provided an opportunity for personal growth, a way to experience an all-female context that helped them overcome previously negative perceptions about such environments. For many of the other female informants, the social benefits of participating in single sex ensembles were cited as an obvious strength—

sometimes anticipated and sometimes not. Several females spoke of a sisterhood, "total girl time," and how the group provided a "chance to talk about girl things." As Rhonda emphasized, "We can talk about anything we want [in all-female]. There's no weird male-female thing going on... Those kinds of [all-female] conversations can happen *and* they do!" Carla made a point of mentioning that in her group everyone always takes their shoes off during rehearsal. "In co-ed I wouldn't take my shoes off!" she added.

Males, too, were keen to endorse the benefits of the single-sex social environment. Derek's comparative comments below are telling because of what they expose about the perceived relative simplicity of single-sex settings, and, in Derek's case, the heteronormative assumption that single-sex settings would not contain "drama."

> I personally prefer being in an all-male group after being in both. In terms of camaraderie, it's just easier to sit around with a bunch of guys and have a good time. All these other groups talk about this drama they are having with people with both sexes, intergroup whatever, or if you have an all-female group—I'm not going to comment because I don't want to be sexist—but that happens. It's much easier to be a bunch of guys and just hang out and enjoy what we are doing and make these crazy cool harmonies and chords.

In addition to invoking what can be perceived as the privileging of male experience (discussed more below), Derek's comment about "drama" in co-ed groups paralleled a theme that arose in several interviews. As a single-sex group member explained, "Co-ed is too much like a family. I don't think a family can function that way. There's too much drama." A co-ed group member, on the other hand, found the heterogeneity healthy: "Co ed causes more drama, but that's not necessarily bad."

Sexual Dynamics

Reflecting on her initial aversion to being in an all-female group, Julie remarked, "Now I realize it was dumb fears. Now I see the co-ed groups and the problems." The problems alluded to by Julie—the drama in co-ed groups mentioned by several of our informants—invariably reflected the workings of heterosexual desire. As professors in music education concerned primarily with making connections between school music and lifelong music-making practices, inquiring into the sexual relationships of collegiate a cappella participants was not part of our original research agenda. By our second or third interview, however, it became abundantly clear that sexuality was an unavoidable aspect of the singing experience in collegiate a cappella. Chelsey, a member of an all-female group, for example, explained that she preferred co-ed not because of the sound "but because there were males." Miranda, an all-female member from a different group, was even more emphatic: "I enjoy the company of men!" As a result of such comments, we subsequently included questions intended to figure out sexual dynamics within groups. As we discuss below and in the next chapter, the nature of many (but not all) interviews tended to reflect a heteronormative frame.

The presence of sexual tension in collegiate a cappella groups is not surprising given the number of hours members spend together and the intimate nature of collegiate a cappella singing. The possibility of sexual relations among members was clearly recognized by everyone interviewed. As one informant put it, "becoming close is only natural"—although, as another informant remarked, "you know too much to be interested." Relationships were not, in themselves, an issue. Sexual relations were generally only problematic when inevitable "breakups" threatened group cohesion and functioning ("fortunately we haven't had to deal with a breakup; in 2007 they did"). Groups approached this issue in one of two ways: they had rules—written or unwritten—against what almost every interviewee referred to as a form of incest (e.g., "we have a rule: no [group name]-cest"; "we don't outright say it—that's a *Pitch Perfect* thing"), or they accepted sexual relationships as inevitable (e.g., "it has happened; it's awkward"; "stuff has happened, but people have handled it maturely"; "it happens every year"; "it can be open as long as it's not *too* open") and expected members to put the group's interests ahead of their personal issues and desires ("I would like to think that any two people who were thinking about it would discuss it beforehand"). From what we could gather from several of the interviews, individuals did in fact prioritize group interests, as there were very few reports of anyone ever leaving a collegiate a cappella group over interpersonal conflict (e.g., "breakups happen; nobody's quit the group over it").

Male-female relations in the collegiate a cappella world exhibited several facets beyond the potential for sexual relations within co-ed groups. For example, most all-male groups had a formal or informal partnership with an all-female group (but the reverse was not always true, as all-female groups outnumber all-male groups). In some cases there were references to sexual aspects of such partnerships, in that males and females could pursue sexual relations without the potential for interfering with group chemistry in the event of a breakup, but more often, the partnerships reflected a form of platonic friendship that could exist without the backdrop of competition that might occur between a single sex and co-ed group ("our [male group] just gets along better with all-girl groups"). These male-female group partnerships were described by some as "brotherly and sisterly," reflecting a mutual appreciation of being in a single-sex group where one had familial-like responsibilities to look out for one another. A homologous situation appeared to exist within the co-ed world as well, where there were comments about groups being "possessive"—that is, members wanting to protect each other. In the words of one co-ed music director, "even though there is sexual tension, you look out for one another. [The group is based on] a model of a family. Older people look out for younger. The boys look out for the girls and vice versa."

What went largely unspoken, save for three interviews, was the possibility of sexuality that wasn't heterosexual in nature. On this point, our positionality (Roger straight, Brent gay) came into play. Due to common stereotypes that associate singing with femininity and gay males, we were attuned to the possibility of gay relationships within all-male and co-ed groups. (About collegiate a cappella audiences, one of our informants stated point blank, "gay guys and girls will show up: that's the arts"). In our research, however, we did not find anything particularly unexpected. Although we did find one all-male group with three openly gay males, we did not encounter in our interviews anything to suggest there were more gay males (or females) in collegiate a cappella than any other walk of life.

Roger's heteronormative frame came into play while interviewing members of two all-female groups. In one interview with two members of an all-female group, for example, where Roger was discussing how some of the all-male groups had a sizable female following, one of them remarked, "We have a certain following too, but it's not as large." Roger subsequently failed to pick up on the shared giggles that followed, which were in reference not to a male following but a female one. In another interview, Roger made a comment about how some of the co-ed groups have rules against "[group name]-cest" and how this wasn't likely an issue in an all-female group. The two informants politely (and patiently) explained that they too had a "no [group]-cest" rule and that the previous year they had had two people dating who were very discreet ("it was professional"). It was clear in both interviews that the all-female groups in question were very sensitive to the presence of sexual desire within their single-sex environments and how this had the potential to destabilize group functioning.

Gender Asymmetries

> They're like the Beatles. They're like the Backstreet Boys of BU.
> —Comment about a prominent all-male group

> Last year the Bubs asked us to be the guest group for their concert. They had two concerts in the same night, both of which were paid tickets. The Bubs had three encores!
> —Comment about a prominent all-male group

> All-female isn't going to have male groupies. It doesn't work that way.
> —Observation by an all-female informant

In addition to generally possessing the highest status in the collegiate a cappella world, the members of all-male groups also tend to enjoy aspects of privilege not common to females or most male members of co-ed groups. One of the most obvious examples of this was found in audience attendance. Whereas the co-ed concerts we observed drew maybe 200–300 people at most, it was not uncommon for major all-male groups to draw over a thousand people, almost all of whom were young females whose audience behavior was reminiscent of female fawning for major male popular music performers (e.g., Beatlemania). As one informant put it in reference to the all-male group on campus: "you can't find an auditorium large enough for them."

- *In [X] Auditorium (absolutely packed; approx. 1000)*
- *They perform like they rehearse; they convey "male sensitivity"*
- *A very female-looking audience (the look and the sound: lots of hoots)*
- *EWF tune—lots of falsetto; applause was deafening*
- *They sing w/more energy, closer harmonies than other groups; more intricate arrangements*
- *A very different vibe from other concerts I've attended: more of a presentation/performance than a sharing*
- *Almost a Glee parody feel (lots of "ba daht")*
- *Very polished performance (and performers; more like music majors even though they aren't); programming is very deliberate (inc. slow songs)*
- *Limited but effective choreography*

(Field notes of an all-male performance, April 30, 2011)

Adoration was not restricted to just the top groups, however. As two members of a lower profile all-male group explained, males who sing, especially in a group setting, experience heightened sexual interest from females. As one of them described how girls always want to give you their number, the other chimed in, somewhat apologetically, with, "It's like shooting ducks in a barrel." The two went on to share a story of a mutual female acquaintance who said to them, "I didn't think your friend was that attractive until I saw him on stage."

The perceived desirability of male singers was not simply the fabrication of narcissistic males. The females we interviewed were almost universal in expressing their desire for male collegiate a cappella singers ("Yes, it's attractive!"). Two members of an all-female group were forthright, saying that males on stage are "sexy." As Beth explained, "We call them a cappella goggles. Because it's true. I think it's a pretty normal thing that if a man can sing, it's pretty attractive. I mean, I'm a big musical theatre kid, so if a guy can sing and he is straight, that's a pretty exciting time for me. Because it never happens!" In fact, almost all of the stories we heard on the issue of the sexy male singer came not just from females but from females who were clearly self-aware and, in many cases, quite familiar with issues of gender equality, as in this observation from Miranda:

> I know that personally I am attracted to men—especially as a musician—but probably even if I weren't a musician. I find it very attractive when men are able to sing well and so I was asking [my friend], "How does that fit into patriarchal systems? Why aren't men attracted to—like—why don't they flock to the women's concerts?" And I don't know if this is entirely true, but she suggested that historically maybe women are expected to be talented artistically, or to be at least capable and sufficient. Maybe that's one look at it. Whereas for men it's like something they're not expected to do.

Interestingly, there was a marked difference in the desirability of males in single-sex versus co-ed groups. As Mallory, a co-ed member stated, "When you see them singing, there is something unique about an all-male group." When asked, "What about guys in co-ed?," one informant replied, "It's just different." Alex, an informant from an all-male group, explained the difference in desirability as a reflection of the differing natures of all-male and co-ed groups:

> I think there is sort of a connotation that co-ed groups are kind of dorky, or that there is a bit of like they get around and sing and they are just choir kids all over again, whereas there is definitely the view that groups of guys that get together and sing all have like suit jackets and like they dress really cool and they are like cool people... [It's] like we're rock stars.

Alex went on to explain that the possibility of being desired was part of the motivation for wanting to audition into an all-male (rather than co-ed) group, although in his response to a question about why members liked singing in the group, he also expressed a slight uneasiness about motivations that derive from sexual desirability rather than the joys of musical participation itself.

> I definitely think it's for the attraction factor. I think it's because women think singing is attractive. But I would hope that some part of them is also really invested in singing and that they really enjoy that and will definitely use this format as an outlet for that. I think there are a lot of people in [the group] that enjoy music fundamentally but don't want to sing in the [campus] choir because it's not the cool thing to do. But they'll sing with [this group] because they are a bunch of super cool dudes that sing.

The overtness of the "attractive male singer" that translated into a larger fan base for all-male groups and that resulted in male sexual advantage (because apparently males in all-male groups were, unlike those in co-ed groups, assumed to be available) was just one manifestation of privilege. Another aspect of this privilege was found in the passive-aggressive tensions that existed and were, strangely, promoted among all-female groups. As Rhonda explained, "[this group] and [that group] are supposed to hate each other because we're both all-female. Everyone is always comparing us: Who's cooler? Who's hotter?" These kinds of comparisons were largely self-induced by females, often to the bewilderment of some male informants (e.g., "all-female groups always want to know who we [the all-male group] think is better") who became de facto authorities of judgment. One female member explained that males don't feel competition in the same way. She admitted to being very competitive against other all-female groups, apologetically offering, "We don't collaborate as much as I would like. There's that *girl* thing.'" Another female informant insisted that woman on woman competition wasn't unique to collegiate a cappella: "It's part of our society."

The attractive male singer and inter-female competition alone, however, fail to adequately account for the overwhelming advantage male singers enjoy in the collegiate a cappella world. One of our interview questions asked informants to offer explanations for the differences in status between all-male and all-female groups. Julie pointed out the confidence she observed in all-male groups, especially in comparison to her own all-female group, about which she commented, "We stand in a circle and look like losers bopping around." Or as another all-female member commented about all-male performance practices, "As females we can't do that." One interview with two members of an all-female group is worth quoting here at length for what it reveals about gender asymmetry in collegiate a cappella.

Chelse:	Male groups can do a lot more. They can take girl songs and turn them into silly goofy kinda skit-style stuff. They always seem to have so much more energy—I don't understand it, it drives me crazy.
Beth:	They just have better lung capacity. I don't know what it is.
Chelsey:	It just infuriates us.
Beth:	It's absolutely the most annoying thing in the world.
Chelsey:	Because we want to be as interesting to watch and as great to listen to. For example, the MIT Logs are by far one of the most entertaining groups.
Beth:	They had 4,000 people at their concert in December. They had to turn away people.
Chelsey:	The thing is, guys can do that; they can be like goofy and stupid and people find it endearing, but yet when girls do it gets *really* awkward.
Beth:	Yep, because you can't tell whether they are being serious or not. Whereas if guys try to do something silly it's assumed that they're trying to be silly…
Chelsey:	It's like they're trying to be silly.
Beth:	Whereas if *we* do something silly! Were they? *Were they?* OR were they going for something and it didn't really land? So guys can do the sexy thing very well because it's always a little bit assumed as a joke, and if we try to do it it's like, *What are you trying to do?*
Chelsey:	Yeah, like put your skirt back on or stop! Why are you shimmying or stuff like that.
Beth:	Yeah. There are certain like double standards but also—they *are* better than us at some things and I cannot figure out why. If we could figure out why, that would be the, you know, secret recipe. And then female a cappella could take over the world!

Notably, the level of gender "wokeness" seemed appreciably higher among females in all-female groups than those in co-ed groups (perhaps in part because the status superiority assumed by the latter). Many of our informants from all-female groups were aware of their gendered subjugation. Some informants used words like "patriarchy," and we heard comments such as, "we hate the system that gives privileges to males." In one case, a person's choice of college attendance was determined by their desire for co-curricular singing coupled with an awareness of inequality in the a cappella world.

> I was in an all-female a cappella group [in high school]. There was an all-female, co-ed, and an all-male group at my school and the all-male group got a lot of

recognition even when they weren't the best group and so that was something that always frustrated me and I was like, "I really don't want to go to a school where there's an extremely prominent all-male group." I wouldn't want to go to Tufts or Brandeis, those big-name all-male a cappella groups. I can't be competing with these people for the next four years. It's just going to drive me crazy.

In some cases, female informants were aware of their inability to adequately critique the problems: "I wish I was a WAGS [women and gender studies] major so I could analyze this better. I don't feel I can analyze this very well. I know there is so much analysis of gender that could be made of the a cappella world, but I'm an environmental science major." In other cases, there was an added frustration for those who recognized the double hit that all-female groups face: not only do they have to endure the double standard of performance practices and expectations but pragmatic concerns very often force them to perpetuate the system that is the source of their oppression. As Miranda and Leslie explained, while there may be solidarity to be found among sisters, the reality of public performance requires they rely on the male groups that are the source of their opprobrium:

> **Miranda:** I think it gives us the shared bond of really hating that external reason and the way it gives additional privileges to any group with a male in it, be it an all-male group or a co-ed group.
>
> **Leslie:** But I don't think it erases it because for our mid-semester concerts who do we invite to come sing with us? All-male groups, because that's who's going to attract the audience.

Curiously, all-female groups in some cases were forced to rely on all-male groups rather than co-ed groups because co-ed groups were often reluctant to associate with an all-female group. As one co-ed informant remarked, "If all-female groups ask us [to share a concert] we won't do it because we're not going to have as much fun."

The lack of awareness of male privilege among members of all-male groups was both surprising and, to us, disappointing. While many males recognized (and appreciated) the perceived desirability of male singers in all-male groups, many failed to fully grasp the difference between performance ability and sexual desirability. Informants of all-male groups would boast about how many requests they receive to be a guest group for performances. They recognized the financial benefits ("groups want to do concerts with us because it is profitable") but then equated such benefits with assumed superior performance ability—an equation that seemed to them based on the presumption of meritocracy: their group was the best because they worked the hardest. Rarely did males recognize the structural forces propagating their advantage.

Status, hierarchies, gender, and sexuality are part and parcel of the collegiate a cappella world. As the comments of our informants make clear, these dimensions of collegiate a cappella are not ancillary to, or outside of, musical experiences but are integral to them. Many questions arise in response to the inequities documented in this chapter, perhaps the most central being how collegiate a cappella creates and sustains gender and sexuality hierarchies—a topic we explore in the next chapter.

4

Sustaining Inequality through Singing

"Your girlfriend will love us"

To claim that collegiate a cappella is gendered is an understatement. Not only are groups divided into all-male, all-female, and co-ed but the musical arrangements, the social interactions, the costuming, and the performance presentations all reflect "traditional" gender binaries and roles. Given that our previous scholarship and research has focused primarily on the sociality of music making, issues of gender and sexuality in collegiate a cappella should not have come as such a surprise to us. Spending substantial time observing rehearsals and interviewing, however, convinced us unequivocally of the absurdity of speaking of "nonmusical" or "extra-musical," as if social matters can be conveniently divorced from the making of music. Where people are involved, norms of gender and sexuality (to say nothing of race and class) are involved and perpetuated.

Recognizing that our initial investigation lacked specific questions about gender and sexuality, we reconnected with two informants who self-identified as gay during our initial interviews. Josh, a cis-gender gay male, was the president of his co-ed a cappella group. Alex, a gender-queer-gay-male (the only "out" gay male in his group's history to that point), had been the president of his all-male group. Their perspectives, coupled with the views of our other informants, helped us examine how sexuality and gender intersect to reinscribe male privilege and heteronormativity.

We approach this chapter from our positionality as educators with a commitment to gender and sexual equality. Our discussion situates collegiate a cappella within and against the field of music education but does not presume that collegiate a cappella participants themselves are under any moral or professional obligations. Rather, we theorize collegiate a cappella through the lenses of heteronormativity and performativity and an historical consideration of Greek life (i.e., Greek letter societies) in order to demonstrate and "make sense" of gendered practices in singing, from which educators may wish to draw implications.

Scholarship from Choral Education

Literature in the fields of choral conducting and music education is primarily situated within a Western historical context of colonization. According to Gates (1989), men dominated choral singing in colonial New England. The role of singing in the lives of men and women and, in particular, the role of male singing in aspects of culture and society (Jones 2010) have been documented and explored, with special attention paid toward the attitudes and perceptions of males (Carp 2004, Castelli 1986, Mizener 1993, Power 2008, Roe 1970, Sweet 2010) as well as the experiences of males in choir (Adler 2002, Faulkner and Davidson 2006, Freer 2006, 2009, Harrison 2007, Keating 2004, Kennedy 2002). Similarly, the acknowledged decline and absence of males in Western choral singing has been a popular topic (Demorest 2000, Freer 2007, 2010, Koza 1993, Lucas 2007). Also prevalent in choral and music education literature are discussions of sex and gender stereotyping (Harrison 2007, 2008, Hawkins 2007, Maidlow and Bruce 1999, Millar 2008, Viggiano 1941), the negative effect of school choirs on females (Koza 1992, O'Toole 1998), the identity formation of males (Freer 2009, 2010, Parker 2009)—especially in regard to the changing voice (Freer 2008)—and the benefits or challenges of single-sex choirs (Carp 2004, Jackson 2009, Jorgensen and Pfeiler 2008, Patton 2008, Reed 2004, Zemek 2010). Over the past decade, topics surrounding sexuality (Palkki and Caldwell 2018), voice variants classification (Bond 2018), and the experiences of transgender singers (Bartolome and Stapleton 2018, Palkki 2015, 2017, Palkki and Caldwell 2018) have also emerged.

The intersection of masculinity and sexuality in collegiate a cappella complicates simple claims and theories about group singing, especially those claims that suggest males are reluctant to sing due to perceived threats to their masculinity. Assuming that heterosexual attraction is linked with masculinity—which is asserted in much of the music education literature as undermined by singing—what then explains how male singers in collegiate a cappella, especially those in all-male groups, are viewed so consistently as sexually desirable (and hence masculine)? How can singing be viewed simultaneously as both effeminate and masculine? How can male singers be pejoratively described as gay while simultaneously serving as the object of female heterosexual desire? Conversely, feminists might ask why perceptions of effeminacy are viewed negatively or with derision? If singing involves associations with femininity, why is this not similarly viewed as sexually desirable (thus inspiring the fandom of males)?

Gender and Music

To suggest a link between music and gender is hardly novel. Susan McClary's (1991) book *Feminine Endings: Music, Gender, and Sexuality*, while not the first statement on the subject, was arguably the contribution that brought to prominent attention the then-provocative idea that music was not as innocent or autonomous as often assumed. Our research suggests that, in accord with much extant literature, collegiate a cappella participates in the (re)production of gendered and sexual norms and their attendant inequalities. We noticed several aspects of this, especially with respect to perceptions of sonority and its connection with desired sounds, preferences for same-sex and co-ed social environments, heteronormativity, male privilege, and male sexual advantage.

The segregation of singers into same-sex and co-ed groupings can be understood as stemming from a number of factors, most notably the historical origins of collegiate a cappella in all-male Ivy League settings—but most of these factors do not help to explain the desirability of tessitura and sonority reported by many of our informants. For our female informants to suggest that a good arrangement can mask the undesirability of an all-female sound raises the question of whether humans have a natural proclivity for lower sounds. Our suspicion is that sonority preferences among our informants are more likely tied to collegiate a cappella's evolution during the 1990s into a pop music "cover band" practice. That is, the norm for most collegiate a cappella groups today is for voices to emulate and substitute for the vocal and instrumental parts of popular music (hence the more recent term "contemporary a cappella"). Without electronic manipulation (something that would undermine the premise of natural voices), most female voices cannot imitate the bass range (examples like Sweet Honey in the Rock excepted) typically found in popular music tunes. This is likely why we heard comments about the necessity for male voices and the need for all-female groups to try to mask the lack of bass sounds.

This explanation about sonority preferences does not adequately account for all aspects of sex segregation, however. Although males can use falsetto to cover higher parts in the sonic spectrum, for many males this comes with a change in vocal quality. Hence, it is often advantageous, whenever possible, to have a "high tenor" or two in the group. But this raises the question of why all-male groups wouldn't just include a female or two (as, for example, the group Pentatonix has done), because if the rationale for group hierarchies in the collegiate a cappella world is based on sonic rather than gendered reasons, then there is no justification for not having a female or two in a group. Alex's thoughts about this are particularly revealing and worth quoting at length:

> Occasionally, self-identified women with very low voices have asked to sing with our group because they think that we are the coolest—because you know we have this reputation and following. We bill ourselves as "the premier all-male a cappella group" on campus and these experiences have prompted us to consider what would happen if an individual who identifies as male, but biologically was female and very much carries that voice part wanted to be a part of our group? Would that work for us? Would we audition in terms of voice type instead of sex? That's something that our group has struggled with a lot and, like, depending if you are going through treatment that will also change things because of hormones, so where do you go with that? Eventually the decision of the group was to continue going for biologically male voices because apparently "that's based on physics" and it was decided that that is what our group is based upon. Although I would argue that it is rooted in heteronormativity and a cis-gendered male culture more so than having a deep voice.

Alex went on to clarify that having a trans-person, even one with a desirable voice, "wouldn't fly probably." He acknowledged that, while the group had tried to convince itself of its openness and inclusivity, auditioning decisions inevitably rationalized the continuation of the all-male norm.

Heteronormativity and Performativity

> One is not born, but rather becomes, a woman.
>
> — Simone de Beauvoir

Inspired by Alex's comments above, we consider in this section how gender and sexual norms are perpetuated through the musical and social practice of collegiate a cappella. As researchers, we were in different places in our thinking about heteronormativity and aspects of performativity when we started this project nine years earlier. However, as the analysis of our data took shape, we could not help but theorize the historical legacies of gender norms on our participants and their actions today. For readers less familiar, we first provide some contextualization and conceptualization of the terms "heteronormativity" and "performativity" and explain their relationship to collegiate a cappella within the structures of campus life. Heteronormativity is a term that typically refers to the interdependence of gender and sexuality (Ingraham 1994). Gender is assumed to be a binary category, with sexual attraction normalized as directed at the opposite gender. Nonheterosexual structures of desire, such as homosexuality, bisexuality, pansexuality, and asexuality, are thus marginalized and perceived as deviating from the heterosexual norm. Subsequently, nonheterosexual structures cannot exist without reference to heterosexuality and gender as a binary category (Jackson 2006). "The heterosexual norm" thus refers to a hegemonic form of heterosexuality that can be described as "traditional gender arrangements and lifelong monogamy" (Jackson 2006, 105). This does not mean that all heterosexual relations represent a norm. For instance, there are forms of heterosexual nonmonogamous relationships (e.g., cheating on a spouse) that are also stigmatized and associated with immorality. These, however, are generally regarded as flaws in character rather than an affront to the natural order of things.

Heteronormativity originated in queer theory as a critique of liberal feminist movements and theories that reproduce and reify gender as a binary category and a heterosexual norm. The term was first used by Michael Warner in 1991,[1] although predating Warner were similar concepts in feminist lesbian theory. Adrienne Rich, for example, called this phenomenon "compulsory heterosexuality": a "political institution" that is the basis of "male domination" (Rich 1980). Similarly, Monique Wittig (1989) coined the term "heterosexual contract" to describe patriarchal gender relations as heterosexually structured and, consequently, gender and sexuality as inseparably intertwined.

Arguably, the most well-known idea conveying the logic of heteronormativity is Judith Butler's (1990) "heterosexual matrix," which represents a social and cultural system of order, thinking, and perception that forces humans into the form of physically and socially distinct genders (bipolar gender system). The matrix is illustrated in three parts: (1) you have a body with a fixed sex (that is either male or female), (2) upon which culture builds a stable gender (either masculine or feminine), (3) which determines your desires (toward the "opposite" or "same" sex). These binary distinctions of gender are hierarchically positioned, the desire of which is targeted at the opposite gender and thus forms gender and sexual identity. Butler states that we should not accept that any of these parts follows from the last. Our bodies do not determine our genders, and neither do our genders determine our desires. In essence: (1) you have a body, (2) you may perform an identity or identities (and this may change over time), and (3) you may (or may not) have desires (and these may change over time), and all of this may be fluid.

---

[1] Warner first used "heteronormativity" in the introduction to a special edition of the journal *Social Text* (1991) titled "Fear of a Queer Planet." In the article, Warner demands that sexuality become a category of social analysis. Warner also advocates that heteronormativity be explored as an underlying power structure. By doing so, heterosexuality can be described by the concept of heteronormativity as a structure of power throughout social and cultural spheres.

One way of understanding how something as seemingly innocuous as collegiate a cappella might participate in the perpetuation of gender inequality is through Butler's (1990) concept of *performativity*.[2] In her landmark book *Gender Trouble*, Butler uses the concept of performativity to help explain how both sex and gender are socially constructed through performance. Building off the work of Simone de Beauvoir, J. L. Austin, and Michel Foucault (among others), Butler argues that the repetition of particular behaviors helps to construct what is often taken by many people as natural or "real" about sex and gender. Butler writes, "[W]hat we take to be an internal essence of gender is manufactured through a sustained set of acts, posited through the gendered stylization of the body" (Butler 1999, xv). Moya Lloyd describes Butler's use of performativity this way: "Gender isn't what one is, it's what one does. It's produced through repetition through time… The gendered self has no ontological status apart from the acts which compose it. It has no abiding essence, except as the effect of performative enactment" (Lloyd 2005, 25). Put differently, performativity is a concept that seeks to explain how repeated doings become internalized as the right way to do things. In de Beauvoirian terms, one becomes a woman by doing what are generally taken to be what women do. If one extends this idea to the collegiate a cappella world, males and females make seem natural and biological that which is socially constructed through the ritualistic performance of norms.

Butler's prose doesn't always make it easy to understand performativity. For example, when she writes that "the 'coherence' and 'continuity' of 'the person' are not logical or analytic features of personhood, but, rather, socially instituted and maintained norms of intelligibility" (1990, 17), we interpret this as meaning that society has many generally accepted notions of who a woman is and should be based on what are perceived as essential features of being anatomically female. Butler argues that these notions are not biological, but rather, the effect of historically derived social and cultural interactions. When she writes, for example, "there need not be a 'doer behind the deed,' but that the 'doer' is variably constructed in and through the deed" (1990, 142), she attempts to make clear that she is not talking about an embodied individual who dresses or acts in a particular way and thereby becomes a woman, but rather, that the always already normative societal enactments of doings are what construct commonly accepted notions of what females believe about themselves as females.

---

[2] For those new to the word, it is worth noting that "performativity" has been used by other authors in ways that differ from Butler's usage.

One of the key points about performativity is the distinction between a performance as a bounded act and performativity understood as the "reiteration of norms which precede, constrain, and exceed the performer and in that sense cannot but be taken as the fabrication of the performer's 'will' or 'choice'" (Butler 1993, 24). No matter how much freedom and agency one wishes to claim or imagine, for example, one cannot be whoever one wants to be when it comes to matters of sex and gender. This is to say that a given individual cannot just unilaterally, through an individual action (i.e., performance), change what are, to borrow Michel Foucault's terminology, long-established "regimes of truth." "Doing gender," Lloyd explains, "is culturally compulsory; it is a form of reiteration vital to viable subjectivity" (2005, 138). Gender and sexuality, in other words, cannot be unilaterally determined. Any individual act that deviates too far from accepted norms will not register as legible. "For a performative utterance to succeed, it has to conform to an iterable model" (Lloyd 2005, 137). We would argue, then, that collegiate a cappella practices, while they involve "performances," are performative to the extent they (re)iterate norms of who males and females are and "should be."

Performing Gender in Collegiate A Cappella

A consistent theme among many informants we interviewed was that "men who do music who are not effeminate are sexy." When asked to further explain this frequently reported theme, Josh struggled to come up with an explanation:

> It's like, "This person is so artistic and sensitive and he actually likes women. Oh my god, he's a one-in-a-million—what a catch!" And I guess it must be the mindset. *But I don't know.* Even gay men find straight men in a cappella to be attractive, so I guess that doesn't really make sense. I don't know why this is inherently more attractive... It is to me, too. And I'm gay!

As one of our heterosexual female informants helped to clarify, "Girls don't think of singing as gay; it's other guys who do." And yet, the sexual desirability of males sometimes differed between co-ed and male groups, with the latter usually perceived as more desirable.

We would argue that collegiate a cappella provides an intriguing example of the complexities of gender performativity. Some informants, for example, noted how the attire of many all-male groups affirmed traditional notions of masculinity more effectively than that of the co-ed groups. When asked why the males in his all-male group were perceived as more desirable than those in the co-ed group, Alex replied,

Because they look great with all the jackets and stuff. It's a good look and that certainly has an amount of appeal to me. I like the fashionable aspect of it. Whereas [the co-ed guys are] adorable and they wear bowties and suspenders, but it's not so much the sleek blue steel look of the sports coats.

Josh affirmed this belief. He noted how the nature of the fan support for males in his co-ed group differed from that of the all-male group: "there were plenty of guys who could sing great [but] who weren't sexy because they weren't wearing a blazer."

Sartorial practices certainly reflect one aspect of masculinity, but it would be a mistake to assume a monolithic version of masculinity among male singers. Rapkin, for example, described the all-male group The Hullabahoos (a group that started as a "bad boys" alternative to the upstanding Virginia Gentlemen) as the "anti-Beelzebubs" (2008, 56). Just as the Hullabahoos took pride in their flag football team as an expression of male physicality, one of the all-male groups in our study took pride in their group doubling as an intramural soccer team. In terms of heterosexual desirability, it appeared to us that what mattered most was not the emulation of any particular kind of masculinity (fighter or lover, to borrow a dated example) but that males in all-male singing groups were perceived as "fair game" for females.

Several informants made much of the difference between the "super cool dudes that sing" (i.e., singers in all-male groups) and the "dorkiness" of singers in co-ed groups. As Josh lamented, "co-ed is not sexy"—a comment that speaks to both opposite and same-sex desire. Josh's perspective was not universally held, however, as we witnessed many examples of the sexual desirability of co-ed males, though certainly this was not nearly as dramatic as the overt displays of adoration shown by females toward males in all-male groups. Images invoked by the phrase "The Backstreet Boys of BU" (Chapter 3) certainly appeared to ring true. It is not an exaggeration to compare what we witnessed at some all-male concerts to Beatlemania or female fans at Elvis concerts—phenomena that serve as to challenge assumptions in the school singing world that traditional masculinity is challenged or undermined by singing.

In terms of audience attendance and behavior, the contrasts between all-male and all-female performing events could not be more pronounced. Top all-male groups drew over a thousand people (paid), whereas some all-female groups were lucky to approach a hundred (unpaid). All-female groups that desired larger audiences made sure to share a concert with an all-male (or at least co-ed) group. Whereas males were the target of female affection and adoration, the reverse was not true. As made clear in our data, almost all participants were well aware of this asymmetry. Some females were bothered by it ("double standards"; "guys can get away with being silly"), whereas others simply accepted it as the way things were ("girls aren't funny"; "guys won't go crazy over a female a cappella group").

Heteronormative and Male Sexual Advantage

Recall that heteronormativity expresses a basic structure of social units and institutions such as kinship, marriage, and family relations as well as relations of friends, people at work, and so on. Simple actions by colleagues, such as displaying photos of spouses and families on work desks or wearing wedding rings, are markers of these social units and institutions and communicate values and expectations that regulate behavior and police expectations. The world of collegiate a cappella is unmistakably structured on a number of heteronormative values that parallel society at large. As described in Chapter 3, our informants assumed many things about the merits of single-sex groups versus co-ed groups. One prevalent assumption was that single-sex settings would not contain what they described as "drama" (in reference to heterosexual romantic encounters). Many informants from same-sex ensembles reported the comfort they felt singing in the company of men or women because they could, for example, just "pal around" or enjoy "total girl time"—comments that underscore the heteronormative assumption that same-sex attraction does not or could not exist. It should be noted, however, that in our data, there were at least four examples of groups where "drama" did result from same-sex attraction. These incidences, however, do nothing to erase the overwhelming prevalence of what is sometimes described as "heterosexual privilege" found in the world of collegiate a cappella.

Very few of our informants explicitly referenced "heteronormativity," but consider these keen insights from Alex:

> Just recently I saw on a friend's Snapchat story the posters for auditions this year say: "Your girlfriend will love us." And my first thought was, "I'm abroad for one semester and we've completely forgotten that it's not just guys who like women who sing in this group." There are a lot of times when we are just hanging out or are rehearsing that it can get very heteronormative. Although they can be inclusive when I'm around, it's not like their first thought is to think that maybe someone might be in the closet in that group and so then they create this culture where heterosexuality is the norm and it completely stifles everything else.

For participants like Alex, something as simple as a poster advertising group auditions functions not only as a regulatory mechanism that serves as a "dividing practice" (Foucault 1982) but as a constant reminder that heteronormativity is performed through almost every aspect of social life.

Our informants appeared to enact many heteronormative practices that affirmed stable notions of gender and sexual relations between members and between groups. All-male groups often held mixers with the all-female groups, for instance, where they would sing for one another and party, sometimes with the expectation of "hooking up." Co-ed groups, on the other hand, didn't typically participate in such mixers with all-female or all-male groups. It could be that the potential for opposite-sex coupling already exists within the composition of the co-ed group—even if such coupling was (and is) generally frowned upon for its potential to destabilize the harmonious functioning of the group. Regardless, it is interesting to consider how the performative effects of collegiate a cappella activities help to sustain heteronormativity, as Alex's comments make abundantly clear:

> I think it's telling that our major hangouts are with the all-female group, especially when the other openly gay singers are in the co-ed a cappella group. It might be nice for someone like me in an all-male group to have a mixer where we might get to hang out with the co-ed group where there are actually guys and people that I might be interested in in terms of a relationship, but it's fine. Let us just go talk to women and eventually hook up sometimes. That happens. But, obviously it can't for me.

Our data largely echo Rapkin's discussions of male sexual advantage in collegiate a cappella. Rapkin, for example, observed a female fan at a Hullabaloos concert who proudly referred to herself and her friends as "Hullabahos" (2008, 62). Rapkin also noted how male singers would sometimes pick out a female in the audience and pretend to draw a box around them, assuredly knowing that they would have a sexual encounter with that person. He concludes, "On campus—though it's crass to say—a cappella will get you laid" (Rapkin 2008, 7). For our informants to use phrases such as "a cappella goggles" (in reference to females viewing male singers attractive) and "shooting ducks in a barrel" (in reference to how easily male singers could hook up with girls) corroborates Rapkin's observations. It also underscores how collegiate a cappella participates in both the performative enactments of heteronormativity and the asymmetrical balance in the power relationships between males and females.

Greek Life: A Speculation

Part of Butler's argument is that gendered norms and practices are part of ongoing iterability; there is no original. To avoid the nihilism of determinism without the possibility of agency, Butler suggests that resistance can exist in the gaps between iterations. The image often provided to make sense of this is that of the palimpsest. More recent theorizations in the field of posthumanism have invoked slightly different metaphors to explain agency and determinism as they relate to norms and practices. Karen Barad (2007), for example, has advanced the notion of "agential realism," which she supports with, among other ideas, the concepts of "intra-action" and "entanglements." The basic idea (not that Barad's or Butler's ideas are basic) is that the binaries upon which so many beliefs about being human rest are fictions that need to be exposed in order to rethink agency, ethics, and so on. Methodologically, Michel Foucault provided one possible approach to doing this through what he called, after Nietzsche, *genealogy*. This "history of the present" works backward, attempting to identify what Butler might describe as the gaps between iterations, seeking to expose what Nietzsche called "descent" and "emergence." We make no grand claims to have engaged at the level of a Foucault, Butler, or Barad, but we do think it helpful to consider how collegiate a cappella participates in the iterability of long-standing gendered practices as part of what is typically called "Greek life."

Today, a good deal of social life at colleges and universities is structured around "Greek life," which on many campuses includes Greek housing. For example, Gettysburg College, where Brent works, has seven sororities and nine fraternities. Seven of the fraternities have residential houses on campus, yet none of the sororities have houses, raising the question of why are there no sorority houses at colleges like Gettysburg?[3] Because many colleges and universities like Gettysburg didn't admit women until the turn of the twentieth century, the established houses created during the college's early years helped firmly perpetuate a system of advantage for males. Purchasing property, moreover, was a right restricted to men well into the mid-twentieth century. Even after women had the right to purchase property, very few had the economic means to acquire parcels of land without the assistance of men. As a result, sororities continue to operate from a material position inferior to that of fraternities.

Although an examination of housing issues helps to explain some of the asymmetrical privilege of fraternities and sororities, this does not explain why or how Greek life came to dominate the US college experience in the first place. The first secret societies on American college campuses are reported to have

---

[3] According to Penn State's Greek life page, the reason is based on economics. Properties are expensive to maintain, and after the Second World War—when universities in the United States were rapidly expanding to accommodate the influx of veterans returning home from war and attending college through the new G.I. Bill—universities offered affordable communal living options within the residential life structure to sororities and fraternities. This allowed organizations the opportunity to rent space instead of having to maintain and pay taxes and upkeep on older properties.

emerged around 1750, a time, it must be remembered, when formal education was restricted to males. Following the US Revolutionary War, *literary societies* came into existence at nearly all colleges and universities in the United States. Often called Latin societies, these formal organizations often met in large public assembly rooms and competed against each other in debate, discussion, and presentation of poems, essays, fiction, or original composition. As Winstead (2013) documents, singing was a ubiquitous aspect of these groups and organizations. Societies were typically associated with a political, social, or religious set of beliefs and they adopted mottos in Greek or Latin that connected to their missions. The Latin societies figured prominently in the development of the modern version of fraternities and sororities and thrived until about the time of the American Civil War when fraternities became secretive and private, allowing for the preservation of pre-Civil War race and class values (Harding 1971, Turk 2004).

The expansion of sororities in the 1880s was tied to the difficult objective of demonstrating the viability of the education of women. Proving that women could perform academically as well as or better than men while maintaining Victorian ideals of womanhood was a tall order. For many wealthy families willing to support their daughters' educational endeavors, sending them away to a co-educational residential college was often perceived as risky. Sororities were viewed as helping to ensure high academic standards among their members—a way of ensuring equal standing on campuses. Sororities were also formed to help monitor the social activities of members, thus assuaging fears that women not under parental care might be tempted to engage in behavior thought to be inappropriate or immoral.

While admissions at many higher education institutions had opened to women through the latter half of the nineteenth century, student organizations were still free to restrict membership. Sororities were thus essential as one of the only organized opportunities available to women. Intense curriculum and mandatory religious involvements during this period limited leisure activities for both men and women, but the social sororities and fraternities began a tradition of interaction that mirrored the aristocratic social gatherings of the colonial era. Individual sororities on campuses would often pair up with a fraternity, reminiscent of the all-male/all-female a cappella group pairings described in Chapter 3. These "sister" or "brother" organizations often worked together on philanthropic endeavors and provided social events for singing and dancing after meetings were over.

Even for those today who do not participate directly, Greek life has become a central part of the "college experience" for many students attending US institutions. Regardless of actual membership, Greek life is omnipresent on many campuses, which varies from institution but is often cited as being in the 35–40 percent range. Three percent of the American populace are reported to be current or alumni members of Greek organizations. Greek organizations are reported to be the largest network of volunteerism in the United States. Notably, however, members of Greek organizations have been identified as primarily white and primarily from higher socioeconomic backgrounds. In addition, sororities and fraternities enjoy a statutory Title IX exemption, meaning that institutions are under no obligation to ensure gender equivalency. It is fascinating also to consider that every US president and vice-president except two have been Greek life members, 63 percent of presidential cabinets since 1900 comprised Greek life members, over three-quarters of the US congress are reportedly Greek life alumni, and, prior to the confirmation of Brett Kavanaugh in 2018, forty of forty-seven US supreme court justices have been Greek life alumni.[4] In addition, an overwhelming majority of CEOs and top executives of American businesses are Greek life alumni.[5]

Relationships between Greek life and collegiate a cappella are speculative, but intriguing. That all-male and all-female groups mirror Greek life in so many ways is hardly coincidental. That these normalized gendered structures are so unquestioned and underscrutinized is, for us, rather shocking. But then again, history performs itself so subtly that the present inevitably becomes accepted as the natural order of things and people rarely imagine that things could be different. What is important to recognize, we think, is how something as seemingly innocent as collegiate a cappella participates performatively in the reinscription of, among other social facets of life, inequalities of gender and sexuality.

Male Privilege in Choral Settings

The suggestion of gender inequality in and through musical practices is hardly new. Feminist scholars in music education have been pointing this out for decades. Patricia O'Toole (2000), for example, compellingly argued that, despite the repeated claims of music educators that teaching music is just

---

[4] Maria Kornikova provides more detailed figures on the matter in *The Atlantic*: https://www.theatlantic.com/education/archive/2014/02/18-us-presidents-were-in-college-fraternities/283997/, accessed June 1, 2020.

[5] Other quick searches on the internet reveal lists of powerful alumni. See, for example, https://www.businessinsider.com/famous-fraternity-sorority-members-2017-10; https://www.usnews.com/news/education-news/articles/2017-12-04/is-greek-life-worth-saving, accessed June 1, 2020.

teaching music, the making of music is inherently gendered. We take this to mean both the sense of double standards for men and women and the sense that the experience of music making differs for males and females. O'Toole writes, "Men are more frequently judged on their merits or potential, and women tend to be judged on how successfully they present their femininity (i.e., clothing, hair, make-up, body shape)" (2000, 35). Using the example of the movie *The Full Monty*, she points out the hypocrisy of how, in contrast to the physical standards of beauty to which females are held, males who perform in public are treated as sex symbols regardless of their physical appearance. For females who make music, on the other hand, there is "an anticipation of femininity in the performance" (35). "[W]omen who are too aggressive, overly sexualized, or physically unattractive will meet with resistance and possible dismissal" (35). Males, by contrast, can be "sensitive, aggressive, passionate, and pudgy" (35).

O'Toole suggests that music making is performative in the sense that it participates in reproducing inequalities in society. She urges educators to more fully consider their involvement in sustaining such inequalities, arguing that schooling holds at least some potential to resist and disrupt such inequalities. To the extent they recuse themselves from such responsibilities by hiding "behind a claim of neutrality" (38), music teachers are guilty of failing in their professional obligations. We share O'Toole's critique when she writes: "By not including gender, we fool ourselves into believing that boys and girls have the same experiences in music when clearly, they do not. More importantly, not including gender in music matters continues to support existing identity positions that tell boys they are special and girls that they are ordinary" (35–36). The phenomenon of collegiate a cappella provides, we believe, compelling evidence for why music educators should care about gender and sexuality in the classroom.

Historically, sex-segregated singing practices were quite common, on grounds ranging from the cultural to the religious. We would argue, however, that sex segregation becomes more complicated in settings such as schools and universities, which are most often predicated upon a kind of ecumenicalism. Except in cases of explicit mandates that might require sex segregation (e.g., Orthodox Judaism), religious and cultural practices are supposed to be bracketed out of public institutions and not used to justify sex segregation. While most sports practices remain almost universally segregated, this is usually accepted as a physical and pragmatic necessity. Sex segregation in public institutions—and we would argue that most private universities are only private in an economic and governance sense, not because of any reluctance to embrace "publicness"—raises questions about its necessity or desirability.

One frequently invoked argument in favor of sex-segregated singing in schools is based on what Koza (1993) called the "missing males" problem (for a thorough review of male choral participation issues, see J. Williams 2011). That is, some choral educators believe that sex segregation is a desirable strategy for addressing insufficient male choral participation, even though there has yet to be any empirical research that supports arguments for sex segregation in schools (Zemek 2010).[6] Interestingly, of course, few in the choral world acknowledge the presupposition that the need for male-female "balance" is largely predicated on the nature of the repertoire—that is, the motivation for additional male singers isn't actually based on an altruistic desire for equity in the choral room but on professional self-interest in wanting one's ensembles to perform particular repertoire and have it sound a particular way. This self-interest is masked by an educational justification that claims that all students benefit from performing SATB (art music) repertoire.

O'Toole (2000) has argued that responses to the so-called "missing males" problem have had several unfortunate effects. The paucity of males in the choral classroom has sustained twentieth-century American discourses that link male singing to effeminacy and homosexuality (see e.g., Koza 1993) while simultaneously privileging male singers in various ways, such as having lower standards for entry into top performing ensembles compared to females and treating male singers as special. As Zemek (2010) concludes, the underrepresentation of males in school choral ensembles "perpetuates unequal power relations and fosters the continued neglect of female and gay male students' educational needs" (17). We might add, however, that it is not the underrepresentation of males itself that produces negative effects, but rather, music educators' (well-intentioned) efforts aimed at reducing the imbalance.

---

[6] Marcia Patton (2008) offers an argument for sex-segregated choirs in an article published in *Choral Journal*, based on her reading of Louann Brizendine's (now discredited) book, *The Female Brain*. Patton writes, "If we believe findings that communication, connection, emotional sensitivity, and responsiveness differ in female and male brains, we should advocate for separate boy and girl choirs that complement brain strengths as well as everything that constitutes the human voice" (68). Such arguments, while well-intentioned, fall prey to the kind of "is-ought" fallacy whereby biological differences (by which we mean actual differences, not those imputed to exist through behavior attribution) are understood as providing empirical evidence upon which to determine action. Even if female and male brains could be shown to be different (beyond something as simple as size or shape, which in and of itself would tell us little about how brains work), it simply would not logically follow that boys and girls should sing in sex-segregated settings based on physical brain differences. From a philosophical standpoint, differences in brains (or anything else, for that matter) could provide a strong educational argument against sex segregation.

Singing, Gender, and Collegiate A Cappella

As described in the beginning of this chapter, singing has sometimes been viewed, historically and cross-culturally, as a "masculine" activity. And yet, many prevailing norms in American culture over the past 100–150 years situate singing, especially group singing, as gay and/or effeminate. Collegiate a cappella is a world where traditional masculinity is expected and rewarded, and femininity is regularly criticized, silenced, and rejected. As Lamb states, "dominant discourses make available forms of identity which are tightly circumscribed and which exclude many people" (1996, 125). The dominant discursive and nondiscursive practices in collegiate a cappella have been historically, socially, and culturally constructed by men, leaving little room for women to create their own spaces and identities within the practice. Why else would members of an all-female group so proudly proclaim themselves as "the female group with balls"? We are also reminded here of Valian's (1998) cautionary observation: "Males tend to be perceived as the norm against which females are measured. When one group—say, in this case, men—is the norm, the other group's behavior—in this case women's needs explaining" (26). We contemplated this statement a lot when looking at the data and thinking about various singing practices in and out of institutionalized settings.

Our informants in single-sex ensembles expressed what they felt were many positives about their environment, such as the safety they felt in being able to talk and act in ways they might not when in the presence of a member of the opposite sex, a finding that reveals much about heteronormative assumptions and expectations that exist in society. There was an undeniable sense of bonding and belonging in single-sex groups, reflective of fraternity and sorority (in both the Greek life and non-Greek life senses). Most of our informants viewed this positively (e.g., "total girl time"), although we were struck by how the prospect of participating in a single-sex activity was also greeted with apprehension by a number of our informants. This was especially (and for us, surprisingly) the case for females, many of whom were "terrified about getting into an all-girl group" and would say things like being "girled out."

We had conducted many interviews prior to encountering Rapkin's book *Pitch Perfect*, but we could not help but be struck by how similar our findings were to his: "Mahaela (by her own admission) never got along well with women. But this was different" (Rapkin 2008, 73). To the extent that our informants' participation in collegiate a cappella taught them "how to hang out with girls" (and did the same for males reluctant to be in an all-male environment), one might choose to interpret single-sex groupings in a positive light. One is still left wondering, however, how and why some people continue to feel both safer *and/or* more uncomfortable in single-sex settings—both socially and sexually (as if same-sex desire is invisible or illegible)—than they do in co-ed environments.

To label both same-sex and co-ed ensemble configurations as "collegiate a cappella" is to gloss over the not-so-subtle nuances that lead to vastly different social and musical interactions and experiences. The historical legacy of a cappella singing in Ivy League colleges and the fraternity-sorority system of Greek life may help to explain the continued practice of sex-segregated singing, but what stood out in so many of our interviews and observations was the "givenness" of sex segregation and its attendant hierarchies. Regrettably, we did not ask our informants explicitly about previous experiences in single-sex choral grouping in their secondary school experiences, though a small minority of informants tangentially mentioned instances of singing in all-male or all-female groups in high school. At no point, however, did we note any questioning or objecting to the practice of having all-male, all-female, and co-ed groups, always determined according to cisgender binaries. Some participants may have privately questioned the way that gender overwhelmingly structures the musical experiences of collegiate a cappella, but none of our informants explicitly expressed this to us in their interviews, nor did we glean any sense of concern over sex segregation in rehearsals or performances beyond the hierarchies that exist between differently voiced groups.

Recreational activities differ considerably, in both form and function, from explicitly educational ones, of course. We are not suggesting that collegiate a cappella, a student-initiated and student-run practice not obligated to uphold any sort of public tenets (educational or otherwise), should somehow be regulated by colleges and universities. Rather, our examination in Chapters 3 and 4 is intended to reveal how participation in collegiate a cappella can be viewed as participating in and sustaining gender and sexual inequity in subtle and not-so-subtle ways. For the overall benefit of society, we would hope that educators and others who care about such things might take notice and engage in reflexive processes that question and challenge the many performative practices that sustain power differentials.

Openings for Change

This book was written over a period of time where we witnessed many political changes in the United States. The presidency of Donald Trump helped to move many institutions further to the political right. The performativity of social reproduction and social change, however, works in subtle and mysterious ways. For example, recent calls by faculty, administration, and board of trustees to examine fraternities, sororities, and single-gender clubs at universities are likely to change the participation rates of Greek life on campuses across the United States (Engelmayer and Xie 2018). In response to a report outlining "deeply misogynistic attitudes" and a "sense of sexual entitlement," Harvard University recently barred all single-sex fraternities, sororities, and clubs from holding student group leadership positions, varsity athletic team captaincies, and from receiving College endorsement for prestigious fellowships beginning with the class of 2021, a measure largely aimed at the school's exclusive, all-male social clubs that have been blamed for problems with sexual assault and alcohol abuse (Anonymous 2017).[7] We can imagine that other institutions will eventually follow Harvard's lead, thus, over time, reducing the overall participation in Greek life in American society. Similarly, we can imagine that there may already be singing groups with trans members and groups that are actively attempting to resist the heteronormative culture of collegiate a cappella, thus helping to transform the norms and values that currently result in such overt asymmetries with respect to gender and sexuality.

---

[7] In a GQ article, titled "The Great Ivy League A Cappella Hazing Scandal," Rapkin interrogates Cornell University's decision to disband Cayuga's Waiters, Rapkin's former collegiate a cappella group, for objectionable hazing practices (2017).

5

The Workings of Capital

"If you are a legit institution, you probably have a cappella"

> *I was basically looking at Ivy Leagues and then really small liberal arts colleges that were of about 1500 students. A lot of times they would advertise on tours the number of a cappella groups on campus. One of them I visited said they had the greatest number of a cappella groups per capita. I thought that was weird. I mean—for 1500 kids how many a cappella groups do you really need? But then coming to Harvard—I guess I just assumed they had a cappella. I feel like if you are a legit institution, you probably do.* (Mallory)

As the US college admissions scandal of 2019 illustrates,[1] families with sufficient financial means are prepared to violate the principle of meritocracy in order to ensure their children maintain their social advantage by guaranteeing their attendance at "high prestige" educational institutions. The scandal sets into sharp relief the importance of social and cultural capital. The children of wealthy families do not need to attend high prestige institutions for career reasons (or even educational ones); they need to attend high prestige institutions to ensure the perpetuation of their social positioning. In the United States, the perception of what matters most in education is not *what* you studied in university but *where* you studied. Having been accepted into a particular institution, the next priority in importance for students is to engage in "college experiences" with perceived sociocultural value. As we demonstrate in this chapter, collegiate a cappella has become an unwitting participant in the perpetuation of this kind of social inequality.

---

[1] "College Admissions Scandal: Your Questions Answered," *New York Times*, March 14, 2019. Retrieved from: www.nytimes.com/2019/03/14/us/college-admissions-scandal-questions.html.

The (Un)Cool Factor?

> Where there are nerds, there is a cappella.
> — New York Magazine *article on Googapella (2017)*

> It gives us an opportunity to be part of this phenomenon that's been growing in recent years. And you know, it's a great time to be in a cappella. (Karl)

The first *Pitch Perfect* movie debuted a year after we had begun our research. Subsequent to its release, we asked our informants if they liked or disliked the movie. Reactions were split. Some people recognized the Hollywood tendency to achieve effects through exaggeration (but acknowledged the underlying truths upon which the exaggerations were based), while others were offended by what they considered to be misrepresentations. Of collegiate a cappella's reputation, Rapkin writes, "where does the line fall between serious pursuit and goofy joke? It's blurrier than one would think" (2008, 9). Indeed, if references in pop culture are any measure, there are often polarized reactions to collegiate a cappella. An episode in season nine of the NBC television show *The Office*, for example, titled "Here Comes Treble," featured Andy Bernard (portrayed by Ed Helms) and alums of his fictional collegiate a cappella group from his alma mater, Cornell University.[2] A cameo by Stephen Colbert served to reinforce the ambiguity between cool and uncool. (Was it cool that Andy used to be a well-regarded collegiate a cappella member at an Ivy League school and tragic that he ended up as a lowly, often-frustrated salesperson at Dunder Mifflin, or did his membership in collegiate a cappella portend his future?) Similar examples abound.[3]

It is tempting to attribute mixed reactions about collegiate a cappella to a backlash against its meteoric rise in popularity through the late 1990s and early 2000s. Rapkin, however, suggests that collegiate a cappella has always had its detractors, citing Yale's Society of Orpheus and Bacchus (the SOBs), a group that started in the 1930s with the "expressed purpose to mock the Wiffs [Whiffenpoofs]" (2008, 7). Based on his observations and interviews, Rapkin claims, with perhaps some literary excess insensitive to gun violence, that there are people at Yale who "love and obsess over a cappella" (Yale claims to have over

---

[2] Coincidentally or not, Cornell is also Rapkin's alma mater.
[3] While barbershop and not collegiate a cappella, Jimmy Fallon's recurring group, The Ragtime Gals, on *The Tonight Show*, helps to reinforce the double-faced serious/goofy dichotomy of a cappella singing.

twenty collegiate a cappella groups) and those who "want to take a gun and shoot everyone involved" (2008, 150). One possible explanation for this polarization is what the character Nigel Tufnel in the movie *This Is Spinal Tap* calls the "fine line between clever and stupid." Similar to the veiled meaning behind calling one's group the SOBs, collegiate a cappella group names have a long and storied history of attempts at pun cleverness (e.g., Harvard Law School's "Scales of Justice," Massachusetts Institute of Technology's "Logarhythms"). In whose eyes is the line to be drawn between clever and stupid, cool and uncool?

Rapkin suggests that the turning point in public perception came in the summer of 2007, when collegiate a cappella went from "pop culture curiosity to mainstream pursuit" (2008, 265), attaining a status where he proclaims it (with journalistic bravado) as "one of the most celebrated pursuits on our nation's college campuses" (2008, 5). We are less convinced that collegiate a cappella can claim such lofty standing, but our research does suggest that, at least on some campuses, it has attained subcultural notoriety with considerable clout. Having attained a level of widespread acceptability, it has become, claims Duchan, "a trend that feeds on itself" (2012a, 49).

Practice Theory

[(habitus) (capital)] + field = practice. (Bourdieu 1984, 101)

Our research endeavor was guided by an interest in investigating both the phenomenological "lived experiences" of collegiate a cappella members and the larger structural forces that help to sustain the fundamental belief systems that support various practices. We initially engaged the work of several scholars in "practice theory" (e.g., Ortner 2006, Schatzki 1996, 2002) and have been influenced by them in key ways (most notably Schatzki's notion of practical intelligibility). Based on our previous engagement with the "situated learning" literature (Mantie 2012a, 2012b, Mantie and Tucker 2008, Talbot 2014, 2018b), we also briefly considered the theoretical possibilities of "communities of practice" (Lave and Wenger 1991, Wenger 1998). In the end, however, we concluded that communities of practice was focused more on microprocesses and found Pierre Bourdieu's parsimonious equation of practice as constituted by habitus, capital, and field to provide the analytic framework of best fit.

Bourdieu has become standard fare for many academic fields. Education, in particular, has embraced Bourdieu's theoretical vocabulary for its rich explanations of how social classes and hierarchies are created and sustained through sites of learning. Critics of Bourdieu complain his work is overly deterministic and fails to sufficiently credit individual agency. Supporters, on the other hand, find great theoretical power in his central concepts and argue that Bourdieu does recognize agency, albeit in a form delimited by structural forces. One of the difficulties in utilizing Bourdieu's theories and concepts is that they tend to operate at a high level of abstraction, which enables them to be used across many contexts but at the expense of explanatory power.

To be clear, our familiarity with Bourdieu's work functioned analytically both *a priori* and *a posteriori*. We were, in other words, well aware of Bourdieu's concepts when designing the study and the interview protocol, and these concepts sensitized the eyes we saw through when observing groups (e.g., noting the sense of self-assuredness among so many collegiate a cappella members). We subsequently considered our interview and observation data primarily in light of a Bourdieusean frame whereby *practice* is understood as constituted by *habitus, capital*, and *field*.

Practice

A seemingly simple word, the precise meaning of "practice" quickly unravels when one contemplates the intersections of its use as both noun and verb.[4] What is the relationship of the *practice* of fly fishing or astronomy to *practicing* the piano or free throw shots in basketball, for example? For practice theorists, *practice* is about seeking to explain human action—what Theodore Schatzki calls "a temporally unfolding and spatially dispersed nexus of doings and sayings" (1996, 89). For some theorists, practice refers in broad strokes to a domain of activity (e.g., astronomy), but for theorists in the Bourdieusean tradition, practice usually refers more precisely to "activity bundles" (Schatzki 2002, 71), such as, in our case, all the micro and macro sayings and doings that comprise collegiate a cappella. Where one practice ends and another begins is rarely clear; however, many activities belong to more than one practice, and some practices involve sub-practices. As Schatzki summarizes:

> a practice is a temporally evolving, open-ended set of doings and sayings linked by practical understandings, rules, teleoaffective structure, and general understandings. It is important to emphasize that the organization of a practice

[4] In both a sociological and philosophical sense, this resonates with Michel Foucault's theorizations of "discipline" (most notably in *Discipline and Punish*).

describes the practice's frontiers: A doing or saying belongs to a given practice if it expresses components of that practice's organization. This delimitation of boundaries entails that practices can overlap. A particular doing, for instance, might belong to two or more practices by virtue of expressing components of these different practices' organization. (2002, 87)[5]

As is likely obvious, collegiate a cappella involves sub-practices, such as selecting and arranging of music or choreographing performances, and exists within a larger framework of musical practices, such as singing, popular music, and so on. This raises issues of the familiarity or "expertise" necessary to engage in a practice. As Schatzki points out, someone "can recognize flute playing and even respond appropriately to it without being able to play the flute… But although such propositional understanding might enable them to call the same behavior flute playing as others do, it will probably not enable them to join in with responses to such playing" (1996, 93). This is to say that to be a central participant or "actor" in a practice requires meeting a threshold of insider knowledge.

The salience of practices is that they help to provide a coherent analytic for understanding action. As Schatzki points out, "actions presuppose practices" (2002, 96), which is to say that most human activity is, on some level, purposeful and not random. Within the a cappella rehearsals we observed, singers were found to employ a similar language and set of vocabulary specific to a cappella. Words such as "MD," "perc," and "choreo" peppered the rehearsal. The rehearsal structure itself followed a routinized set of actions that often involved gathering, socializing, warming-up, singing something familiar to build confidence, working through something new, and ending with something that left participants wanting to return. Collegiate a cappella can thus be viewed as a "practice" insofar as a set of actors consistently employs specific intelligible actions. Put differently, there is a high degree of agreement on what to say or do in any given context.

Habitus

To say that actors in a practice share a strong sense of what to do in a given situation is not to suggest that actions are so habitual or routinized as to be mindless. For Bourdieu, the improvisational nature of action delimited by a

---

[5] Schatzki goes on to distinguish between what he calls "integrative" practices such as farming, cooking, and so on, which are complex and join many different ends and actions, and "dispersed" practices, such as flute playing: "In contrast to the doings and sayings that compose integrative practices, those composing a dispersed practices of X–ing are usually linked by a practical understanding of X–ing alone" (2002, 88). Collegiate a cappella would thus be classified as a dispersed practice in Schatzki's formulation.

set of norms is explained by *habitus*, a term that has been used (and, in the opinion of some, abused) by many scholars and researchers to help explain how given practices reflect underlying historical and structural conditions. Bourdieu defines habitus as "acquired dispositions, the durable ways of being or doing that are incorporated in bodies" (Bourdieu 1993, 15). This notion of embodiment loosely echoes Michel Foucault's notion of *discipline* ("disciplined bodies," Foucault would write). Not to mistake physicality for what Bourdieu means by "incorporated in bodies," but in our research, we were frequently struck by how often the deportment and conduct of collegiate a cappella participants exemplified similar patterns of observable behavior, reflecting—as we later discuss—similar habitus.

In *Distinction* (English publication 1984), Bourdieu articulates how habitus helps to determine what he describes as "lifestyle." In the context of our study, people involve themselves in collegiate a cappella for nonprofessional reasons (e.g., our participants frequently used the word "extracurricular" to explain how they regarded their involvement). This is to say that the decision to join and remain in a collegiate a cappella group represents a lifestyle choice—except that, according to habitus, this lifestyle choice is delimited by a person's biographical context, that is, a choice where not all options are equally weighted and where an actor is unaware of what may be influencing their seemingly independent choices. At a most basic level, this is hardly a profound observation. One's upbringing builds capacities and awareness of some things and not others, as is clear in this reflection by one of our informants:

> I wanted to follow in [my mother's] footsteps, and so when she went to college she joined an a cappella group and she would tell me all about how much fun it was and how she loved it so much, and my brother, who went to Tufts, was very good friends with someone who went to Wellesley and was in an a cappella group there, so I would every so often hear about that, because I was friends with her little sister…

One can hardly participate in a practice one knows nothing about. As evident above, one's life history serves to create the menu of options from which to choose as well as to increase the odds of one choice over another. In the strictest sense of habitus, however, an actor is usually unaware of how their history has influenced their choices, which are assumed to be wholly autonomous (i.e., it is forgotten history). Our informant's ability to articulate reasons for becoming involved is therefore not really an example of habitus in the Bourdieusean sense. However, our observations of the informant made clear that a cappella was *embodied* in a comfortable, taken-for-granted way that was more than likely beyond her level of awareness. She knew exactly what to say and what to do in collegiate a cappella contexts and spoke about her experiences as if all people could just successfully audition into a collegiate a cappella group if they wanted to.

Field

A field, according to Bourdieu, is a goal-oriented setting in which actors and their social positions are located. "In order for a field to function, there have to be stakes and people prepared to play the game, endowed with the habitus that implies knowledge and recognition of the immanent laws of the field, the stakes, and so on" (Bourdieu 1993, 72). The position of each particular actor in the field is a result of interaction between the specific rules of the field, as well as an actor's habitus and their capital (social, economic, and cultural). Fields are constructed according to fundamental principles of division (the division between male and female for example) or organizing "laws" of experience that govern practices and experiences within a field. The fundamental principles in one field are often irreducible to those underlying another. Actors enter into a particular field not by way of explicit contract, but by their practical acknowledgment of the stakes implicit in the very "playing of the game."

Collegiate a cappella does not operate in a vacuum. Bourdieu's concept of "field" led us to think about the ways in which collegiate a cappella exists within a wider world of musical practices. At times, Bourdieu has compared "field" to a game such as soccer. The analogy here might be understood on various levels. For example, one might view the totality of collegiate a cappella practices as the game, whereby various groups represent players or perhaps whereby something like the ICCAs represents a league within which various groups play. The game, and its "rules," thus represents a particularized, narrower understanding of collegiate a cappella, somewhat removed from wider life contexts.

Alternatively, the concept of field might see collegiate a cappella as operating within the game of extracurricular activities on campus, especially those under the auspices of a given college's "student activity council." The rules in this case might refer to how various groups leverage resources and participants within the "college experience." Utilizing the metaphor in yet another way, collegiate a cappella represents one player within the wider game of musical practices—or perhaps *recreational* musical practices. This latter distinction takes on a great deal of importance, both conceptually and theoretically, insofar as it helps "place" collegiate a cappella in various contexts. For example, understanding the field in this sense helps to explain many of the frustrations expressed by our informants regarding collegiate a cappella's relationships to various institutions and stakeholders.

Capital (social, cultural)

> The reproduction of social capital presupposes an unceasing effort of sociability, a continuous series of exchanges in which recognition is endlessly affirmed and reaffirmed. (Bourdieu 1986, 250)

In the sociological essay "The Forms of Capital" (1986), Bourdieu presented four categories of capital—economic, social, cultural, and symbolic—in order to explain the resources available to an individual that have value within a given sociocultural context. Economic capital refers to money, property, and other assets; social capital refers to networks of influence or support based on group membership, such as family, friends, or other contacts; cultural capital refers to forms of knowledge, educational credentials, and skills; and symbolic capital refers to socially recognized legitimization such as forms of honor and prestige. Bourdieu links these various forms of capital by illustrating how social, cultural, and symbolic capital convert back into economic capital and can be exchanged within a social "marketplace" or field (1993, 73).

In *Outline of a Theory of Practice* (1977), Bourdieu views each individual as occupying a position in a multidimensional social space, where the individual holds social, cultural, economic, and symbolic capital that can or cannot be exchanged within specific settings. Bourdieu shows not only how individuals are defined by social class membership within their social practices but how each individual is also defined by the kind of capital each individual can articulate and/or access through social relations within the structure of participation.

In *Reproduction in Education, Society and Culture* (1977), Bourdieu and Passeron elucidate the concept of *cultural capital* in order to explain the differences among the levels of performance and academic achievement of children within the educational system of France in the 1960s. They demonstrate how being born into specific families exposed certain children to forms of cultural capital that helped advance them over their peers within the educational and social systems of French society. Bourdieu later expanded this idea in *Distinction* as *inherited capital* and *acquired capital*. In other words, just growing up in a middle-upper-class family provides certain children advantages that are not readily available to others. As we demonstrate below, most of our informants came from middle-upper-class families, where economic, social, cultural, and symbolic forms of capital afforded them particular advantages. Their collegiate a cappella participation reflected their social and cultural positionality and served to further their privilege.

"My Mom Went to Vassar"

As lived experience, privilege is often in the eye of the beholder. One person's privilege is another's hardship. In a Bourdieusean approach, however, one methodically and analytically attempts to "locate" people's social positioning based not just on objective financial measures (economic capital) but according to value as embodied in various sayings and doings. For one of our informants to say something like, "if you are a legit institution" in response to inquiries about their college application experience is thus not insignificant. Although not all informants came to university with considerable musical backgrounds, many did—frequently mentioning such things as private lessons, elite competition participation, playing multiple instruments, and so on. Sandra, for example, talked about how while she took classical viola lessons, she also studied fiddling. She also "trained very seriously in opera" her last year in high school, working directly with a professional opera singer. Such stories are important not so much for the developmental competencies implied but for what they communicate about the nature of the households in which the informants grew up. Parental commitment in terms of time, energy, and money suggests not just the presence of economic capital but cultural and social as well.

The privileged habitus of virtually all of our informants came through in many ways, not least of which being the way they spoke about college admissions. Attending college was simply assumed and never in doubt. Informants, for example, provided no qualifiers when discussing their college application thought processes. It was understood that touring several college campuses—invariably high-tuition, high-status institutions—as part of the selection process was not out of the ordinary and nothing to apologize for or feel embarrassed about. This is what *all* people—or at least all "legit" people—did.

When discussing the college application and selection process, informants would say things like how they "only applied to top choices" or how "Brown seemed to have everything." The privilege of choice was ubiquitous (e.g., "it came down to Bucknell or Wellesley"). For one informant the choice came down to Yale and Boston University; he chose the latter because they provided a "full ride." One of the more illustrative cases was Sandra's experience. She recanted growing up presuming she was "Ivy-bound." She always planned to attend Harvard, she recalled, adding, "When you say it out loud, you expect it and everyone around expects it... Everyone knew it would be me." When touring time came around, she found that she absolutely loved Columbia and Dartmouth but wasn't impressed by Yale, Harvard, or Princeton. To her horror she wasn't accepted into one of the Ivys and had to "settle" for one of her "fallback schools." Admittedly disappointed initially, she expressed how happy she was to end up at her current institution: "I'm *so* happy here. It's a great place to be with great programs." In a form of sour grapes she added, "I have lots of friends at MIT and Harvard and I see what their lives are like... I like that I can skate by and do well and have a social life, not being up until five [in the morning] studying."

It would be wrong to paint all participants with the same brush, but it is difficult to ignore the number of informant stories about attending boarding schools, private choir schools, being home-schooled, living overseas as an exchange student, and so on. It is also difficult to ignore the mentions of educational attainments and professions of family members (e.g., "a sister at Princeton," "my mom went to Wellesley," "my mom went to Vassar," "my parents went to Brown and played in the orchestra there," "my brothers are at Tufts and Williams," "my dad went to BC," "my mom did an MBA at University of Michigan," "my dad is a doctor and loves musicals," "my mom did Broadway in New York," and "my dad is a pianist who went to Eastman").

One of our areas of inquiry addressed the evaluation criteria and processes by which people were accepted into groups. This line of questioning was, at first, just a curiosity derived from our interests as music educators wondering about gatekeeping and coordination practices, given that there can be a dozen or more groups on some campuses. In short order, however, our concerns expanded from logistics to the social reproductive aspects by which audition practices help to militate against diversity.

The specific details of audition practices vary from group to group and institution to institution. In general, it is helpful to remember that groups tend to be twelve to fifteen members in size, with this number broken down approximately evenly across years (e.g., freshmen, sophomores, juniors, seniors). This means that each year a group will typically have to "replace" approximately two to four graduating seniors. Occasionally there are mid-year auditions, but in most cases, the week or two around the start of the fall semester is the primary audition season. Having advertised through various media and the university's "activity fair," groups schedule a first round of auditions, usually on a given evening. Audition routines vary (we heard stories that included drawing pictures, telling jokes, etc.), but candidates are usually asked to match pitches, sing a song of their own choosing, and are sometimes taught a short section of a song to see how well and how quickly they learn it and how well they blend with the group. Groups then shortlist and notify successful candidates for a second round, after which they typically make final decisions. Some groups then have elaborate rituals for notifying their new members.

Where things get more complicated is on campuses with multiple groups. We heard a few stories of antagonisms, poaching, and other duplicitous practices, but we also learned that at several universities, the group presidents had something of a coordinating council (not unlike Greek life councils) to help ensure that competition over members did not result in disruption and disharmony. As one group president at a large institution put it, "groups have to organize or there'd be chaos." In cases where candidates were selected by more than one group, for example, a candidate could be given the option of joining the group of their choosing. In other cases, however, group presidents might "negotiate" who wanted whom. As discussed in Chapter 3, this was not always a negotiation between equals, as higher-status groups often had greater leverage, resulting in a situation where the "top" groups managed to take the "top" singers.

Precisely what constituted a "top" singer in the minds of a cappella participants interested us. What were the evaluators (usually the whole group, although sometimes only the group's leadership council) listening for—or more accurately, *looking* for? Presumably, groups are always looking for the best candidates. But what does "best" really mean in the context of a multidimensional performance practice like collegiate a cappella, one that involves pitch and rhythm accuracy, part independence, vocal range, blend, and so on, but also physicality ("choreo"), stage presence, and, especially in rehearsals, personability and sociability? Did groups care more about the singing and musical abilities of candidates (keeping in mind that piano playing and music notation reading are considered assets)— or was greater emphasis placed on a candidate's personal attributes?

In the vast majority of cases, audition decisions were based on what was thought best for the group, though we were reminded in one interview that self-interest was not necessarily completely bracketed out of audition considerations:

> Attractiveness was never really taken into consideration when we were putting people in the group, but the petty 19 year-olds in us certainly talked about how cute someone was. It was a big reason that we put a cute gay man in the group when we auditioned one year because I found him attractive and wanted to sleep with him. And then I did. (Josh)

More commonly we heard references to "personality," "fit," and "picking our friends," making clear that audition decisions were not based strictly on musical criteria.

> When we're talking about people, we're not only talking about how well they sing, but how well they fit with the group and how well the group matches their personalities. Just because, who ever said that hit it on the head: *we're picking our friends*—because we are a singing group, but we are also a social group. I remember one year there was a singer that was so amazing, but to put it bluntly, their personality didn't work. When you are spending so much time with people, I think that's more important than you expect it to be. (Anika)

By definition, "fit" means sameness, alignment, and congruence. Not unlike how university music school audition processes help to ensure "whiteness" (Koza 2008), collegiate a cappella auditions help to ensure that participants share similar backgrounds, interests, and awareness (i.e., habitus). In Beth's words, "Sometimes you can just tell that [an auditioner] will fit in with a certain group of people because that's—You know you can just tell. You get that kinda vibe." Consistent with its origins in Ivy League schools, collegiate a cappella remains predominantly a white, middle- to upper-class pursuit. In a sense, this might (*might*) be considered unproblematic—except that collegiate a cappella has very real tangible use and exchange value, and this value is not equally accessible to all.

What we did not detect in any of our interviews was an awareness that "fit" and "picking our friends" might be serving as a gatekeeping mechanism that works against difference. Charitably, this kind of ignorance might be considered benign. The occasional comment, however, reminded us that many informants were blissfully unaware of what *real* difference might mean for social equality. Rob, for example, spoke with pride about his perceived diversity in collegiate a cappella:

> I think a cappella is especially unique in the fact that you are there for a common purpose, but you're all incredibly different people. In a lot of other clubs you get a lot of the same kind of people—people who share a lot more in common. But [our group] is a super eclectic group of people. [One person] is a physics major and, you know, anywhere down to [someone] who does dance and, you know, other things. We have so many different kinds of people in the group with so many varied interests and what not, but we all mesh really well. At least musically we do. (Rob)

Not to discredit the definition of diversity as difference in academic major or personality, but Rob was clearly not recognizing the broader implications of what "different people" might mean. In fairness, his predominantly white institution was not, by most sociological measures, diverse, and so perceived difference in this case may have reflected context. The naïveté of other informants surrounding issues of difference, however, serves as a reminder that few participants are aware of how the operating principle of meritocracy is a façade that masks the reproduction of racism, classism, (hetero)sexism, ableism, and so on.

"They Talk About it a Lot on Tours"

Value, as understood in this chapter, does not exist as naturally occurring. Value is created subjectively (through desire), which then translates into an objectified, market-determined form, known as capital. To illustrate: collegiate a cappella is *valued* by its participants by virtue of their involvement. The extent to which this value is recognized by others is then expressed in terms of "worth" (capital). Neo-Marxists remind us that value can be thought of in terms of "use" and "exchange." A twig lying on the ground, for example, may have little monetary (exchange) value but might be useful for scratching one's back, extending one's reach, building a fire, and so on. As discussed above, Bourdieu's theory of capital is built upon the notion of exchange. Viewed in this way, collegiate a cappella highlights how value is dependent on certain currencies.

One of our early fascinations with collegiate a cappella was its *perceived* value, both among its participants and among the wider social world of music making and recreational pursuits. Thanks to popular media and entertainment, most people have at least indirect knowledge of collegiate a cappella. Our informants' responses to questions about their knowledge of a cappella prior to attending university were telling. For example, Erica mentioned how "a cappella seemed to be *the thing you did* in college if you wanted to sing." Collegiate a cappella clearly has value for participants to the extent they feel it serves a *use* in their lives in terms of personal enjoyment, stress relief, sociability, and so on.

To the extent that their participation translates into other tangible benefits, collegiate a cappella involvement also has exchange value. Within the broader context of the university and society at large, for example, the *social* currency of collegiate a cappella can be highly valued, as evident in this exchange with an informant from an Ivy League university:

I had three phone interviews this week and all three asked me about my a cappella group—and one of them was friends with the one who wrote *Pitch Perfect*, so clearly she was into some collegiate a cappella in some way. I'm very glad it's on my résumé.

Capital—be it economic, social, cultural, or symbolic—functions in the marketplace of exchange. That Silicon Valley has a "techapella competition" among its top-tech companies and that members of this competition vacation together in Tahoe at an event called *Snowcapella*[6] signal to university administrators that a cappella has currency among a desired population. Hence, individual universities find value in collegiate a cappella to the extent they believe it reflects positively on the "college experience" and can be "exchanged" for recruitment.

Chelsey: I had heard of it, but I was like, "oh that only happens in movies or like barbershop quartets," but then when I started touring colleges, a cappella kept coming up, so you know, it sort of became the quintessential college thing to do.
Beth: They talk about it a lot on tours.
Chelsey: They really do, which is funny because it's not something that would really appeal to a whole lot of people, but it's such a popular thing to talk about on tour.

An interesting tension presents itself, however: collegiate a cappella is, on the one hand, "the quintessential college thing to do" that gets talked about a lot on tours; on the other hand, we heard repeated stories (discussed more fully in the next chapter) of the disdain high school music teachers and university professors had for collegiate a cappella. This is unsurprising, of course. Within the context of a university school of music, the *musical* (cultural) currency of collegiate a cappella is, generally speaking, quite low (to the point of being a negative currency). University music units (i.e., conservatories, schools of music) rarely value collegiate a cappella because a rise in the currency of collegiate a cappella and what it represents (amateurs performing popular musics) risks devaluing the cultural capital of the conservatory (professionals performing art music). The more the general public—especially in-demand subpopulations like the tech sector—values collegiate a cappella, the more this potentially undermines

---

[6] Google started Googapella in 2007. It has a very competitive audition process that only accepts twenty to thirty people a year. Similarly, Facebook's *Vocal Network*, LinkedIn's *InTune*, Twitter's *Songbirds*, Dropbox's *Syncopation*, and AirBnB's *Airbnbeats*, to name just a few, unite on stage each year for Techapella, giving techies a chance to put aside their rivalries and instead share in their passion for music. See http://nymag.com/intelligencer/2017/10/silicon-valley-a-cappella-techapella.html, accessed April 15, 2019.

the exchange value of the Western art music of the conservatory. When the dominant classes in society no longer perceive the possibility of exchange in "high art" participation, the value (or worth) declines.

Arguably, one of Bourdieu's most important insights was in demonstrating the association of social status and cultural participation (i.e., cultural capital). Although the specifics of his original research, which showed a relationship between high-status occupations and "high art" activities, has been challenged in recent years (e.g., Richard Peterson's work on *omnivorousness*), the underlying idea has remained remarkably robust, especially in educational circles focused on issues of equity and social stratification (Graham 2009). We were reminded of this consistently in our interviews. Even though we have not conducted longitudinal research to ascertain where all of our informants have landed since our interviews (but see Chapter 8 for selected stories), it seems more than likely that they were on an upward trajectory of social mobility. They may not all be vacationing at Snowcappella, but most are probably found in Bourdieu's class of "distinction." That potential employers would ask about a participant's extracurricular singing activity suggests that the social and cultural capital of collegiate a cappella does possess longer-term value.

Music Education and the Workings of Capital

From an equity standpoint, issues of social and cultural capital raise questions about access and inclusion: who has opportunities to accrue value through collegiate a cappella and who does not? As mentioned in Chapter 1, a perusal of collegiate a cappella websites leaves one with the distinct impression that the demographics of participants do not align with the population at large. Ergo, the value-added potential of collegiate a cappella inclines to those already advantaged—usually white, usually middle-class or higher.

This chapter has been about studying collegiate a cappella as a *practice*, with a focus on how collegiate a cappella participation generates forms of capital that translate into economic capital (e.g., job offers). Although school music education does not have direct relationships with collegiate a cappella, it is nevertheless worth considering the implications collegiate a cappella might have for music educators who care about equity issues, particularly as they relate to capital as theorized in the Bourdieusean tradition.

Scholars writing about music education have considering class-based issues in music teaching and learning from a variety of perspectives (e.g., Bull 2019,

Bates 2017, 2012, Wright 2008, 2010, Hall 2018, Hoffman 2013). The National Association for Music Education position on equity and access states that as a field, "All students deserve access to and equity in the delivery of music education, one of the subjects deemed necessary in federal law for a well-rounded education, which is at the heart of NAfME's stated mission: to advance music education by promoting the understanding and making of music by all."[7] Unfortunately, the word "music" in NAfME's mission statement is left open to interpretation. In practice, the word "music" is enacted not as all musics but as one kind of music (i.e., "quality repertoire"). This is consistent with music education's "democratization of culture" value system, which has, throughout the twentieth century, idealistically sought to ensure that a musical education meant that all people ("music for all") received an education in "cultural" music (i.e., that of the conservatory).

The hostility of the higher education conservatory toward vernacular practices such as collegiate a cappella is understandable. Anna Bull (2019), through her study of youth classical musicians in the UK, points out that the continued institutionalization of classical music is essential to maintaining its value as cultural capital. When society's valuation of high art practices as the sole marker of cultural competence becomes eroded among various power brokers (such as Silicon Valley), the conservatory's currency declines, with little end in sight. What else can the conservatory do but attempt to protect its currency by any and all means necessary? What is less understandable is the hostility, or in some cases antipathy, demonstrated by school music educators toward recreational, lifelong music making practices such as collegiate a cappella. Recall the stories from Chapter 1, where school music teachers failed to support the recreational music interests of Michelle and Zach. Stories such as theirs are hardly exceptional. One need only spend a few minutes examining "mainstream" pedagogical literature in music education to recognize the emphasis—or more accurately, obsession—the profession has on "quality repertoire." Musical subjectivity is consistently and invariably positioned by music educators as entirely dependent on what music is learned and performed rather than on why it is learned and performed. Recreational music making (if accepted at all) is valid only to the extent it involves the right kind of music. Better to not make music at all than to make the wrong kind.

The shared antipathy/hostility of many university professors and music educators toward collegiate a cappella is curious because public schools and

---

[7] https://nafme.org/about/position-statements/equity-access, accessed April 15, 2019.

universities exist for entirely different reasons. While the university music unit's stance may be unfortunate, it is at least potentially defensible based on higher education's claims to specialized knowledge and the fact that students attend by choice. From a Bourdieusean perspective, the sanctity and autonomy of art music (see Nettl 1995, Kingsbury 1988)—the bedrock upon which university music learning and teaching is based—must be protected from the threat of a musical practice that, if it were to be recognized as legitimate, might erode the cultural capital central to the music unit. Public schools, however, exist for reasons very different from that of universities. Compulsory attendance in public schooling is predicated on the assumption that it is in society's interest that all citizens receive a "general education." Fundamental to the function of this general education in egalitarian democracies is the premise that schools should help "level the playing field," thereby setting up the conditions for personal and collective well-being and the possibility of social mobility. Even if this ideal is more myth than reality, this does not absolve music educators of the ethical responsibility of striving for equity and ensuring that all students have at least the theoretical possibility of cultural participation. As music education scholar Vince Bates points out, "rather than consistently or reliably empowering and emancipating children, school music tends to marginalize, exploit, repress, and alienate—reifying social beliefs and structures that uphold economic disparities" (2017, 3).

At one time, claims to high art cultural capital in the original Bourdieusean theorization may have had credence. Today, however, "omnivorousness" is generally accepted as the currency of greatest value. Thus, while art music competency has value as part of broad-based cultural competency, a narrow, exclusive "univore" approach that rejects non-art cultural participation today *lacks* value. As a result, music educators who fail to support and enrich a lifelong approach to music participation—*regardless of repertoire or mode of engagement*—risk harming not only the potential for lifelong engagement in music but the accrual of cultural capital necessary for social mobility. "Music for all," then, can be seen as a value—a particular kind of *music for all*—one that, in effect, deprives people of upward mobility potential.

It is relatively easy to explain away why and how school music educators reflect the value system of the conservatory model of which they are product (see Talbot and Mantie 2015). This does not excuse the need for critical reflection, however. As Ruth Wright concludes on the basis of the Musical Futures program in the UK, "[T]here are big questions to be asked about the type of person suited to becoming a music teacher and the sort of music education and initial teacher education and training they require" (2008, 400). It is intriguing to consider the broader ramifications of arguments for relocating music education certification programs from music units to schools of education, whose values and mission of education "for all"—at least in theory—more closely align with the democratic governing bodies that oversee accreditation.

How, then, might educators—both secondary and tertiary—work toward increased accessibility and equity for all music learners so that social and cultural capital (classical and nonclassical) do not just accrue to the already-advantaged? Would new approaches for the "production" of music teachers represent the potential for new forms of social, cultural, and economic capital among students in their post-secondary learning and leisure time?

6

Agency and Amateurism

"I feel like there's a stigma against anything recreational in music"

I feel there is this tension between [the music school] and recreational musical ensembles. It does bother me when [the music school] won't let us use a rehearsal space but will still include us in their pamphlets or use our name as a recruitment tool. We're listed under "other opportunities on campus," but none of us are allowed to use the facilities in order to practice. There's a really bitter part of me that wants to say, "Hey, if we can't use your rehearsal space, then don't put us in your marketing materials." The fact that I feel that fire every time I see those pamphlets is because I guess in my mind all these musical experiences are kind of the same in that they're valuable and that everybody should have an opportunity to have them. I feel like denying students the opportunity to have those musical experiences is just really vexing to me. (Rob)

Our initial interest in collegiate a cappella derived from a hunch that there was likely much to be learned about lifelong music making by investigating groups of people gathering together of their own volition to sing regularly in "noncredit," self-run ensembles. The majority of people in these groups were, for the most part, making their first independent ("adult") decisions about how to plan their time and their life activities. Put somewhat differently, by studying collegiate a cappella, we suspected we might learn something about the connections between the formative years—school music experiences in particular—and music involvement later in life.

The desire to better understand the connections between school music experiences and lifelong musical involvement arose from considerations of why music should be taught in schools in the first place. Justifications for music study have taken many forms throughout Western history. That music was included in the quadrivium points to a long-standing recognition that there is *something* special about music, even if people still struggle to explain what it is. That music made its way into the curriculum in American public schools in the nineteenth century is arguably attributable more to the efforts of passionate advocates than to a widespread belief that music must be in the school curriculum. (See Kivy (1991) on *desirability* versus *necessity*.) A problem many music educators face today is sustaining the place of music in the schools in a world where nonemployment, "nontested" learning is being squeezed out of the curriculum. We are not suggesting that lifelong participation be the sole justification for teaching music in schools, but it does seem reasonable to be curious about what Stephanie Pitts (2009, 254) calls the "long-term consequences of music education." Justifications need not necessarily include lifelong music making but it does seem problematic (to us, at any rate) that people would spend years learning to make music while at school and then not make any music postgraduation.

The promotion of "carry over," or what might today be called "musical amateurism," was central to the discourse of music educators in the first half of the twentieth century. This discourse largely disappeared in the second half of the century as music educators focused their attention on the value of "aesthetic experience" and began invoking arguments that the goal of school music was not to create lifelong musical amateurs but instead to create future audiences for professional musicians (a subtext implying professional *classical* musicians, as musicians in the popular realm already had an audience). Some music educators may still hold this view despite the implicit condescension ("educate the best, entertain the rest"). It is also curious that lifelong participation does not factor more centrally as a concern of music educators given the growing body of evidence that speaks to music making's health, well-being, and leisure benefits. As Pitts observes, "Given the centrality of enjoyment for adult participants, its absence in much educational discourse on music is striking" (2005, 120).

Exact figures on amateur music making in the United States are extraordinarily hard to come by, but it should be noted that many people do avail themselves of opportunities to participate in music making in their post-schooling years. Not that such organizations/entities are exhaustive, but between New Horizons International Music Association, the Association of Concert Bands, the Yahoo community music band-orchestra listserve, the League of American Orchestras, and Chorus America, one can conservatively estimate hundreds of thousands of people regularly make music avocationally (i.e., as musical amateurs) in large ensembles. This, of course, only accounts for ensembles that closely mirror typical school music offerings and doesn't include the myriad other ways that people make music for purposes of leisure and recreation. Moreover, these kinds of groups do not account for the vast number of what Ruth Finnegan calls the "hidden musicians" (Finnegan 1989). Although there are undoubtedly large numbers of lifelong music makers, one might expect, on the basis of how many students take part in school music programs, to find even more (e.g., millions rather than thousands). For example, if the school music participation rate at the secondary level in the United States is conservatively estimated at 5 percent, crude estimates would suggest that millions of people alive today should be musically active.

For commentators such as Thomas Regelski, the lack of lifelong music making serves as *prima facie* evidence that "what is taught in school has little or no lasting, life-long musical impact on students or society" (2009, 68). Perhaps even more damning has been the charge that, rather than promoting lifelong participation, school music programs may in fact be undermining it. Although over fifty years old, a small study by Lawrence and Dachinger (1967), for example, showed that people who were self-taught were more likely to be lifelong music makers than those who had participated in school music programs. More recently, Lucy Green noted, based on her work with the Musical Futures program in the UK, that "young musicians who acquire their skills and knowledge more through informal learning practices than through formal education may be more likely to continue playing music, alone or with others, for enjoyment in later life" (2001, 56).

In this chapter we consider two primary arguments about why school music programs may be failing to promote musical amateurism: (1) the values of institutionalized music learning and teaching, and (2) the kinds of skills and dispositions fostered by school music programs. In the first section of this chapter we discuss how our informants experienced repeated tensions between the desirability of their musical activity as expressed by those outside music's formal structures and the undesirability of their musical activity as expressed by those inside music's formal structures. In the second part of the chapter we extend our discussion from Chapter 2 on the desire to be good by offering a theorization of what is sometimes called "musical agency." That is, we engage with criticisms that suggest a major barrier to musical amateurism is the kind of musicianship developed in and through school music programs.

Enmity and Loathing

En·mi·ty (*noun*): the state or feeling of being actively opposed or hostile to someone or something. Synonyms: hostility, animosity, antagonism, friction, opposition, dissension, rivalry, feud, conflict, discord.

Loath·ing (*noun*): a feeling of intense dislike or disgust; hatred. Synonyms: hate, detest, abhor, despise, abominate.

One thing we observed over the nine years of our research was a shift in perception regarding a cappella among music teacher associations. This shift is likely tied to the trade industry's influence over these organizations—for example, one can find products and various sheet music for sale at publishing companies' exhibit hall booths and online stores related to a cappella. Events specific to teaching and presenting about a cappella can also now be found at conferences like the American Choral Directors Association. These recent trends point to a shift in public and teaching perceptions around choral music. This is not surprising, as a cappella has entered family living rooms with television shows like *Glee* and *The Sing-Off* and inspired a new generation of music teachers. As Ricky, a recent collegiate a cappella graduate now teaching in a large high school choral program told us,

> Though my music education faculty supported the work I was doing as an arranger and the experiences I gained as a director of [my college a cappella group], I always felt they looked down on the practice and didn't see it as *real* music. But I can tell you, a cappella is where I cut my teeth as a director. It gave me the experience I needed to understand how to approach singers who don't know how to read music well… The a cappella group I started at my high school went from an afterschool club to a full class on my daily schedule that now competes in the ICCA's. My principal and the school love it. The group is good and they have really inspired and elevated the musicianship across the entire choral program.

Comments like the one above display the tension and hierarchy that is felt among expert and amateur singers. Stories like Ricky's show there can be success in merging various techniques and approaches learned in practices outside of the curriculum and that these often connect with students and audiences. As Ricky said, "I just want my students to love singing and to do it with or without my assistance everyday of their lives." When asked how school music programs might do better at promoting lifelong music making, Ricky elaborated:

> Music teachers need to let students know that terms like "music" and "musician" are for everyone. Schools can do better at opening up these definitions. One

barrier that can be removed is the narrow repertoire choices schools of music impose on the audition process. It's simple: let people show you what they can do musically instead of defining musicianship for them before they have even started their journey in college.

The experiences of our informants expose what we perceive as a fundamental problem: historical values and practices in institutionalized music learning and teaching are not generally understood as serving the purpose of lifelong music making. Recreational (or "amateur") music making—celebrated by so many people in society outside the circle of formally trained musicians is, apparently, frequently denigrated by far too many music teachers. Or perhaps more charitably, recreational music making that does not resemble the kinds found in university schools of music is negatively regarded.

Some high school music teachers and university professors, not wanting to appear elitist, resorted to dismissing collegiate a cappella by relying on the well-worn "healthy voice" critique—which, sadly, many students accepted unquestioningly, despite the fact that any kind of singing can be healthy or unhealthy regardless of style.[1] In our observations we noticed some instances of vocal strain, but in the overwhelming number of cases, we observed groups beginning rehearsals with the same vocal warm-up exercises and approaches used in institutional music classes (which is not surprising, since most participants simply emulated what they experienced in their own high school choral or musical theater settings).

Despite many groups engaging in vocal practices virtually identical to the university's choral ensembles, we heard multiple stories about voice faculty deprecating the kind of singing that occurs in collegiate a cappella (e.g., "I'll mention a cappella and my voice teacher will roll his eyes and be like, *that* singing"). Jenny defended her participation, despite accepting the claim that a cappella singing was hard on the voice: "My friend does opera. I guess her voice teacher hates a cappella because it kind of kills the voice. But for me it's the only outlet (unless you join a band) to really sing pop music, and that's what I enjoy." Disparaging remarks were not limited to university faculty but permeated school music teacher perceptions as well. Recall Zach from our first chapter, who shared the following story with us: "My high school music teacher wanted me to be a music major my entire life. But I told her I was in an a cappella group

---

[1] A recent empirical study that included acoustic and laryngoscopic assessments of forty-one college singers found that, although many collegiate a cappella singers *reported* voice problems, there were no differences in *actual* vocal health ("no vocal abnormalities were detected") between trained singers and untrained singers (Baird et al. 2018).

and through clenched teeth replied, '*Oh, that's great.*'" While some participants may have been singing styles that trained professionals consider unhealthy, one is reminded that, across the planet, humans have been singing with many different techniques and approaches for thousands of years. Each of these styles can arguably be done in healthy and unhealthy ways. It seems curious, to us at least, that so many voice teachers would express such disdain for a recreational singing practice that brings such joy to their students. There are countless professional models who have demonstrated for decades that one can sing a cappella music in healthy ways.

Collegiate a cappella has boasted celebrated alumni over the years, from Cole Porter (Yale's Whiffenpoofs) to John Legend (University of Pennsylvania's The Counterparts). Despite such notoriety, the status of collegiate a cappella (discussed in the previous chapter) has never been clear. For the university as a whole, collegiate a cappella groups present a positive image of student life showcased in recruiting efforts aimed at parents—a theme we heard repeatedly from our informants (e.g., "they talk about it a lot on tours"). At the same time, our informants reported that the music unit within the university, *without exception in our interviews*, not only failed to support the efforts of these recreational music makers but worked actively to ensure collegiate a cappella members were not welcome in spaces designated for "music." The comments and actions of music faculty actively discredited or undermined collegiate a cappella activities. As James put it,

> I feel like the college uses us because we sing at the president's Christmas party and all the trustees and faculty see us there and say, "Oh you're so great, the college is definitely doing something good with you guys." We also go around to different schools and represent the college, but then the conservatory says you can't rehearse in their music space… [T]he conservatory is saying you can't use our resources, but then we're going to exploit you for our benefit to make us look good and draw people into the school. It was a factor as to why I came, so I'm sure it affects other people too.

What was so striking to us was the similarity and consistency of the stories we heard at campuses that varied so much in size, nature, and geographic location. According to our informants, the university's music unit's attitudes and actions toward collegiate a cappella approached what could be described as enmity and loathing. One informant explained this as reflecting attitudes of faculty toward student-run activities: "Our music department looks down on everything we do… The faculty is offended when student-run things take priority [in student's lives] over faculty-run things" (Elsa).

One of the most telling responses we heard that sets into sharp relief how the status and value of collegiate a cappella are perceived within the context of noncurricular activities at universities resulted from an innocent question we asked about how an informant's group coordinated their activities on campus.

> [T]here are kind of three parts to your question. There is the inter-a cappella coordination, which is our coordination with the other a cappella groups that exist. Then there is our coordination—or lack thereof—with the music department, and then how we fit into the college. Those are three very distinct things. (Chelsey)

What struck us in our interviews was the accuracy of Chelsey's description. Many of the groups we studied rehearsed in whatever space the university allowed them to book (usually under the rules for student groups booking campus spaces). In our observations, we witnessed many groups rehearsing in inadequate spaces on campus, such as run-down classrooms with poor ventilation and no piano. We consistently heard stories about how university music departments created rules and policies aimed at preventing collegiate a cappella groups from using their practice and performance facilities. As one informant shared, "We would really like to perform in more performing arts venues, not in lecture halls or classrooms. I don't know why we don't have a better relationship with our [school of music]. They've always made it difficult for us to reserve our rehearsal space every year" (David).

Amateurism and Musicianism

> College boys are not professional singers. The Mendelssohn and other choral societies meet a fine public need. But the undergraduate should not be called upon to live up to their standards of excellence. More than that, the college glee club with college tunes and college humor and college tenderness fills a niche in life that is worth the filling. Perhaps it is all sophomoric, it is all adolescent. But this phase of life exists. And however unimportant it may seem musically, nevertheless it deserves expression. We don't know what can be done about it. Harvard started this heresy a number of years ago when it tried to lift the undergraduate singer up into abstract musical realms where he does not belong. Mr. Bartholomew at Yale has made it worse. They are artistically wrong. They don't do the thing that they are supposed to do and the thing which is their only justification. They don't express the life of the college as revealed in music.
>
> — *New York Evening Post*, 1931

> Just what is the purpose of amateuring.. Why go on taking lessons and practicing daily...? Well the answer is obviously nothing like a hope for perfection. Though we amateurs are often driven, and even plagued, by the desire to do it better, the real drive is the sheer love of the playing itself—not just the music but the playing of, with, through, in the music. It is our conviction that if anything is worth doing at all, it is worth doing badly. (Booth 1999, 5–6)

For many academics outside the music world, Wayne Booth (1921–2005) is known today primarily as a literary critic. (Those who teach research methods are likely familiar with his coauthored text, *The Craft of Research*.) Booth was also an amateur cellist, however. His 1999 book, *For the Love of It: Amateuring & Its Rivals*, offers a thoughtful, introspective examination of what it means to pursue music avocationally. He writes, "Over the years all that playing has come to feel less and less like a mere addendum to life, a pastime, a hobby, and more and more like something beyond even an added luxury: it's now a necessity … I'm fully alive when amateuring" (9–10).

Booth's passion is easily understood by anyone who has witnessed dedicated amateurs, which is how we would describe all those we observed singing collegiate a cappella groups. What, then, helps explain perceptions that amateuring is not well-regarded in society? What helps to explain the possible gap between the number of students who study music—typically a freely chosen, noncompulsory subject at the secondary level—during the school years and the number who do not sustain their involvement throughout the life span? Accepting that the love of singing we observed among collegiate a cappella participants is not feigned, and that the passion and dedication among so many of those involved with music groups at the secondary level is not simply an effect of acquiescence to parental imposition, one might expect to witness even greater numbers of lifelong music makers.

Sadly, the empirical research literature in music education offers scant insights that help explain why many people who love making music in their younger years do not sustain their involvement in their adult years. One of the many curious findings to emerge from our interviews was how our informants regarded perceptions of amateur, recreational music making. We heard multiple comments that implied recreational music making was something outside the norm. As one informant remarked, "There is a large stigma against anything recreational in music." Or, as another informant exasperatingly recounted, "I just want to be able to sing out loud and have it not be weird." Comments such as these raise questions about the role of recreational music making in American society. (Why would singing out loud be weird?)

Scholarly commentators in music education have offered a variety of explanations for the lack of ongoing musical participation beyond the school years. Two of the most plausible, in our opinion, are (1) conceptualizing music learning according to a professional paradigm, and (2) teaching practices that fail to develop sufficient musical agency. The first explanation may help to explain the status and perception problem, where recreational music making is regarded as abnormal or undesirable. The second explanation may help to explain why, even when desire is present, music making ceases in the absence of a more knowledgeable other.

"Forget the Musician"

Thomas Regelski (2007) suggests that "[t]he main rival to musical amateuring is the lack of respect given it as a musical practice in its own right. The idea seems to be that musicking [sic] must be supported by years of study and hard work (quantitative criteria), and a single-minded focus on perfection (a qualitative criterion) in order to be valid or valuable" (37). Put differently, society views "amateur" musical activity as a failed attempt at, or an inferior version of, professional music making—which is understood by music teachers as the *de facto* goal of all music learning. This unidimensional professional paradigm renders all other possibilities for music learning invalid. "The primary rival to musical amateurism is the stigma against it as a valid and valuable musical praxis, a stigma that denies its legitimacy as a central curricular goal for music education" (Regelski 2007, 39).

For Rubén Gaztambide-Fernández (2010), conceiving all music learning as professional training can be traced directly to the formal structures that authorize and legitimize: "I suspect that we cannot ultimately question or redefine the purpose and role of music-making in society without questioning and ultimately undermining the very institutions that enable music and music-making to operate" (74). It is the music education profession (writ large) and the structures of training, credentialing, and certification, in other words, that ultimately undermine the potential for normalizing avocational music making by sustaining the hegemony of the professional paradigm.

Regelski (2012) argues that university schools of music militate against avocational involvement due to their slavish perpetuation of what he calls "musicianism," which he sees as the root cause that stands in the way of musical amateurism. For Regelski, *musicianism* (the "tendency to place musical choices and values before or above educational options and values" (2012, 21)) is the result of the social reproductive processes whereby music students become music teachers (see Talbot and Mantie 2015), that is, via university schools of music. Reminiscent of the work of Henry Kingsbury (1988) and Bruno Nettl (1995), Regelski compares entering the musical world of the university to that of the monastery. Music in this space becomes "quasi-sacred, thus venerated 'for its own sake'" (22). The result is music teachers who care more about "music and the limited and basically artificial world of school music than to the musical needs of students or of society… [S]uch teachers serve their own musical needs— needs nurtured by the musical experiences they enjoyed as collegiate musicians and that they earlier experienced in their school music programs, and that they seek to replicate in their own programs" (24). The "out of school musical choices and values" of students, Regelski asserts, are "frequently and decidedly contrary to those of their music teachers" (22). One recognizes this point in the stories of Michelle and Zach in Chapter 1, especially when Regelski writes how "steps are taken to actively be rid of students who do not share the veneration for the music of school music that musicianist teachers demand" (24).

Gaztambide-Fernández (2010) offers a slightly different argument. He suggests that the underlying problem is one of failing to recognize music's social aspects due to an overemphasis on nineteenth-century Romantic notions of individual genius. He writes, "[D]espite the fact that music is fundamentally a social and collective process, we have insisted as music educators on focusing on the individual as the unit of music-making… [T]his almost inevitably leads to notions of talent, individual hard work, and giftedness" (74)—an idea that resonates with Regelski's critique of musicianism, as well as schooling practices that demand individualized assessments documenting "student growth."[2] As a way of circumventing the deleterious effects of emphasizing the individual as the unit of music making, Gaztambide-Fernández suggests "we need to forget the musician" (79) and instead focus on the relationships among music participants and the meanings we co-produce together. Music educators, he writes, "have the power [and the responsibility] to transform how it is we think about musicians" (75).

A Musical Agency Problem?

Philosophers of education have long advanced the view that education's primary purpose is to foster some form of independence or autonomy—what can be considered for purposes here as *agency*, or the "capacity to act." While agency's

---

[2] We might add that, despite the practice of large ensembles in schools suggesting an emphasis on social and collectivist issues, the music education profession's research base has historically been grounded more fully in the scientism of psychology rather than sociology, a legacy that continues to sustain an emphasis on the individual as the unit of music making.

connection with education is most often invoked in relation to general abilities (i.e., agency in life), many people likely intuit the domain-specific nature of agency. One may be agentic in one's professional life and be unable to act in one's personal life, for example. The limits of what constitutes a domain or sphere of action are of course contestable. To accept context as a feature central to agency, however, is to acknowledge its bounded and situational nature.

Some commentators (e.g., Regelski 2005, Jones 2009, Myers 2008b) have argued that the (perceived) lack of amateur lifelong music making is attributable to the lack of *musical agency* (or "musical independence") developed in and through the dominant paradigm of large ensemble music instruction found throughout Canada and the United States.

> [M]usical independence is the *sine qua non* of amateuring. Without sufficient musicianship, fundamental technical command, practice skills, and knowledge of the literature—all used independently of the teacher (or other experts)— amateuring is not likely to develop ... The fact that students in school ensembles are usually *made dependent on the director* for such matters (and more) is already a major reason why, despite the high levels some ensembles achieve, most students do not continue their [music making]... [I]t is what they know, can do, and want to do independently of the teacher or director that facilitates and promotes amateuring. (Regelski 2007, 34, emphasis in original)

For critics like Regelski, musical agency corresponds with the development of musical skills and knowledge thought to be most useful for lifelong music making (e.g., guitar over clarinet, iPad over the clarinet, improvisation over notation fluency, etc.). We do not disagree with the assertion that many school music programs fail to develop sufficient musical independence. If musical agency is not to be conflated with efficacy or competence, however, it must account for the ways in which individuals make decisions based on history, awareness of present circumstances, and future-oriented desires. Discussions of lifelong involvement in music making that focus solely on the development of skills and knowledge in and through school music generally fall short of the mark because they fail to account for how individuals are able to reflect on their musical histories and envision future possibilities for musical involvement.

Sidsel Karlsen (2011) suggests that "musical agency is first and foremost connected to music making, and the physical change and control needed for an individual to produce the desired musical output" (108). We question this restricted definition. While we are inclined to agree that *production* should feature prominently in conceptions of musical agency, the deliberative use of music often transcends the narrow confines of "physical" sound making alone (e.g.,

DeNora 2000, Pate and Johnson 2013, O'Leary and Tobias 2016). This quibble notwithstanding, we agree with Karlsen, with some important qualifications discussed below, that music agency refers, in its crudest sense, to the individual's "capacity for action in relation to music or in a music-related setting" (2011, 110).

In her theorization, Karlsen distinguishes using music for personal purposes (*individual agency*) from using music in the context of other people (*collective agency*). While one can imagine the difference between individual practices and actions and collective practices and actions, such a distinction would seem to reduce to making music alone versus making music with others. This appears to us to position agency as synonymous with efficacy. Although group music making may reflect the truism that "the whole is greater than the sum of its parts" (i.e., collective efficacy), effective action is not how we are proposing to understand musical agency.

We see a major stumbling block in theorizations of musical agency stemming from two issues: (1) the capacity to imagine and apply one's competence over time, and (2) the complicated relationships that exist between solo music making (i.e., by oneself), group music making, and group music making led by an expert or authority figure. The first issue recognizes that, while competence plays a role in agency, it is not the whole of it. As Emirbayer and Mische (1998) explain, agency is better understood as

> the temporally constructed engagement by actors of different structural environments—the temporal-relational contexts of action—which, through the interplay of habit, imagination, and judgment, both reproduces and transforms those structures in interactive response to the problems posed by changing historical situations. (Emirbayer and Mische 1998, 970)

All of this is to say that, if agency is not to be conflated with efficacy or competence, it must account for the ways in which individuals make decisions based on history, awareness of present circumstances, and future-oriented desires. Discussions of lifelong involvement in music that focus solely on the development of skills and knowledge in and through school music generally fall short of the mark because they fail to account for how individuals are able to reflect on their musical histories and envision future possibilities for musical involvement. For example, research has suggested that many graduates of school music programs are unaware of musical options beyond the formal schooling years (Mantie 2013, Mantie and Tucker 2008). Hence, lack of participation in adulthood may not be due to competency or relevance issues but, instead, due to the inability to imagine the application of competencies to future contexts.

The second issue—relationships between various forms of musical engagement—recognizes that music making is not all of one piece. How, for example, does one describe and explain musical agency as it exists for the solo piano player, the string quartet or "garage band" member, and the symphony orchestra or community choir member? Dichotomies of individual and collective agency do not suffice here because they fail to capture how someone might embody a great deal of musical agency in a group setting led by an expert but be completely incapacitated when left solely to one's devices. Conversely, some people generate sophisticated musical creations using digital audio workstations but are incapable of making music effectively with others.

Dimensions of Musical Agency

In Chapter 2 we considered competence and authority in relation to the problem of "being good." Our interest in this issue arose from the student-run nature of collegiate a cappella ensembles and the criticism that school music programs fail to develop sufficient musical agency for people to operate independent of a "qualified" ensemble director. Very clearly, hundreds of collegiate a cappella groups are managing to arrange, rehearse, and perform music to a level sufficient to sustain the interest of their participants despite not having "professional" (i.e., formally trained) musical leadership. While true that the level of musical sophistication and performance in collegiate a cappella varies widely from group to group, even those at the less "musically advanced" end of the continuum (to invoke a not unproblematic evaluation frame) still manage to make music in a way that warrants interest and enjoyment among members. If school music instruction is so wanting with respect to its potential for lifelong music making, what explains the ability of collegiate a cappella to function as a recreational musical practice?

To provide a more nuanced view of musical agency, we draw upon the work of Martin Hewson (2010), who introduces the term "proxy agency" to explain how some people can operate agentically in settings where an "expert" assists in the action. This concept helps to circumvent the problem of agency reducing to mere independent action. Adapting Hewson's conceptual framework, we propose that musical agency may be understood according to three nonexclusive categories: *solo, proxy,* and *interdependent.*

Solo musical agency refers to the capacity to engage in desired musical activities by oneself. This is distinct from Karlsen's *individual agency* above, in that solo agency refers strictly to music making and learning on one's own. Solo musical agency is the capacity to make music without the assistance of someone else, where one also has the ability to go beyond their current musical state through the application of existing knowledge to new musical problems and situations. This requires facility with one's voice or instrument and some fluency of skills that can be drawn upon to scaffold activities leading toward desired individual improvement in light of past, present, and future awareness.

Proxy musical agency refers to the capacity to act on behalf of someone else. This is one of the most common forms of musical agency found in American and Canadian school music programs, where students develop performance skills—often to quite an accomplished level—but the capacity to make music depends almost entirely on the music director or leader. Group members often become quite skilled at executing their individual musical part, performing rhythmically in balance and in tune with others, and with musical responsiveness to the musical directions of the conductor. Importantly, from an agency standpoint, group members join and participate volitionally and usually derive satisfaction from their musical involvement. While initial participation of this type usually (but not always) originates in the school, some individuals extend their participation beyond the school years by joining "recreational" ensembles while at university or in the community, the latter sometimes occurring after a long period of lapsed participation (Pitts 2012b, 2016), indicative of agentic action. The defining aspect of proxy musical agency is that individuals lack the capacity (and often disposition) to act musically on their own or with others in the absence of a more knowledgeable other directing or structuring their musical actions.

Interdependent musical agency refers to the capacity to make music with other people in the absence of a "strong" musical leader. Although this shares affinities with proxy musical agency, a primary difference between interdependent and proxy is that in interdependent musical agency, individuals exercise greater influence on others and meet a minimum threshold of musical independence. Some may possess a great deal of formal knowledge, allowing them to "figure things out" on their own, while others embody a great deal of fundamental musicianship (in terms of competencies such as aural and rhythmic acuity) that allow them to contribute musically with minimal assistance from others. Although a "more knowledgeable other" may in some cases lead the overall efforts and contribute to the overall refinement of musical process and product, individuals with interdependent musical agency achieve a minimum threshold of music making with other people even in the absence of a leader or director.

As is hopefully clear, the distinction between proxy and interdependent musical agency does not reduce to "conducted" versus "nonconducted" groups, because many people (e.g., professional musicians) who make music in conducted groups have the capacity to function in the absence of a conductor and/or can make music in small groups. Although rare, one might potentially exhibit strong interdependent musical agency (along, perhaps, with solo musical agency) but lack proxy musical agency. The three types or categories of musical agency overlap and are present in all people to varying degrees. All people involved with music can thus be described in terms of a multidimensional musical agency profile representative of their capacities in various musical settings, styles, and cultures.

It is also hopefully clear that musical agency (like agency in general) involves a temporal component. The "capacity to act" is an outgrowth not only of domain-specific competencies but of dispositions that involve reflection on past activity, awareness of the present, and imagination of and for the future. Auditioning for a collegiate a cappella group suggests not only "self-efficacy" (in the psychological sense) but also that the individual can imagine themselves as a successful a cappella musician based, in part, on previous musical involvement and awareness of what participation in an a cappella group might require, and in part on the capacity to follow through on all that the often-rigorous audition process requires.

Musical Agency and Collegiate A Cappella

Acceptance into even the weakest collegiate a cappella groups typically requires an audition where individuals must demonstrate such things as tonal and rhythmic competencies and part-independence. While our research did not involve testing or measuring that might determine levels of *solo* or *proxy* musical agency, participation in collegiate a cappella serves as *prima facie* evidence of interdependent musical agency because a cappella singing demands a high level of accountability in interdependent rhythmic-melodic production. Although musical lines/parts are sometimes doubled (and occasionally but less often tripled), there is little room to "hide" in collegiate a cappella.

By their own admission, participants in our study varied considerably in their musical abilities, from relatively accomplished instrumentalists, arrangers, and musical leaders to those who learned music primarily by rote and possessed little technical knowledge of music. Members appeared to be quite conscious of the need for people with specific abilities within the group, something reflected in the auditioning priorities in a given year. For example, if group members know that one, or more, of their best soloists is soon graduating, they might accept someone with a strong solo voice even if that person's formal/technical knowledge of music is weak. Conversely, when group members anticipate their best arranger(s) or musical director will be graduating, they might favor someone with greater formal/technical knowledge but less soloist potential.

Given the range of musical abilities within collegiate a cappella groups, we were curious about the individual learning desires of our informants. One of the questions we asked our informants was what they wished they could do better in music or learn more about. As might be expected, answers reflected what individuals perceived as personal deficiencies. Generally speaking, however, almost everyone desired a better understanding of "how music works." One exchange between two members of a co-ed group highlights that school music teaching may not necessarily be imparting the level of understanding assumed by some music teachers.

> **Elsa:** I think that every music class should do a basic "this is middle C," "this is a C scale." So easy. Everyone should…
> **Adam:** Did you guys not do that in middle school, though?
> **Elsa:** No, we played recorder. I don't know why! We played recorder and—*the glockenspiel!?*
> **Adam:** We did that, too, but in elementary school.
> **Elsa:** Yeah, *but why?!*

From an agency perspective, this conversational exchange suggests that some participants do place their musical interests, activities, and learning in a reflective, temporal context.

We are not implying that the recorder and glockenspiel are without pedagogical merit. The exchange above, however, affirms the criticisms of some commentators that school music instruction may not be succeeding in helping students realize connections between such things as time spent on recorder and glockenspiel and music making later in life, especially if and when instruction fails to include musical understandings, such as middle C on the piano and basic scale construction, that many people consider fundamental to solo and interdependent musical agency.

Admittedly, the responses we received to our question about missing or desired musical knowledge reflected needs and interests specific to collegiate a cappella. It was thus unsurprising that so many participants mentioned music theory as a desired knowledge area, given its centrality to the arranging interests and aspirations of many members.

> I think for me, on the theory side, I wish I had more of a knowledge of how music works. I think I know a bit, but I guess specifically, when I'm doing arrangements

> I know there's a specific sound I want to achieve, but I'm not usually able to get to. It seems to come effortlessly to some people, which is something I try to work on by listening to things. (Anika)

As one might glean from the US College Music Society's "Report of the Task Force on the Undergraduate Music Major," the exact meaning and value of "music theory" is highly variable. The kind of "common practice period" music theory common to typical undergraduate music classes in the United States, for example, is unlikely to support the musical goals of collegiate a cappella members, as evident in a comment from one of our participants: "I also took a music theory class hoping that it would help me with arranging, but I don't think it actually did" (Leslie).

Unfortunately, from our perspective, very few participants whose formal music learning derived solely from school music seemed to express confidence in an understanding of how music works. The arrangers for most of the groups we investigated tended to be pianists and those whose music learning included lessons outside of school. Although responses to questions about lacking or desired competencies for the most part reflected presentism and egoism, the occasional response demonstrated longer-term social concerns:

> I wish I had had real, formal training in music theory, and what goes along with that is that I could play a useful recreational instrument like the piano or the guitar—so that I could sing with people. Like, "Oh, I'll play the guitar. We'll sing a song around the campfire with kids." (Patrick)

In a similar vein to the response above, many informants articulated a desire to possess theoretical knowledge in order to better facilitate music making within their respective groups. Additionally, they also expressed a desire to draw upon such a skillset at any point in their life, leading us to question whether participation in collegiate a cappella leads people to continue making music after graduation.

On Musical Amateurism

Collegiate a cappella represents an intriguing recreational music-making practice for those seeking deeper understandings of musical amateurism. On the one hand, it is easy to dismiss collegiate a cappella as simply a niche activity like Greek life that students regard as part of the American "college experience." As we discuss in the next chapter, there are indeed some who view it that way.

On the other hand, the majority of those we interviewed expressed a good deal of intentionality behind their decision to audition and to devote substantial time and energy to their noncurricular activities. Collegiate a cappella members are not people with professional aspirations, but rather, people who feel the need to participate in leisure-time amateur music making alongside their academic studies. That groups manage to function effectively, both operationally and musically, suggests the presence of agency on a personal level (no doubt the effect of an upbringing with a good deal of social and cultural capital), as well as sufficient interdependent musical agency.

The antipathy (bordering on enmity and loathing) of the music teaching establishment toward collegiate a cappella, if not recreational music making in general, is understandable but disturbing. University music faculty, including music teacher educators, are the products of a system that exists for the purpose of professional training (or licensure, in the case of music teacher educators). Amateurism goes against the grain of the university music school's *raison d'être*. Based on our study, the criticisms of Regelski and Gaztambide-Fernádez would seem to hold all too true. For us, it seems like an egregious blind spot for the music teaching establishment to fail to recognize that a healthy professional "ecology" needs to include a healthy amateur base. The music teaching establishment's focus on professionalism does not need to preclude support for amateur participation. In the sports world, for example, amateur participation is lauded, not denigrated (Conner 2008). While the university sports department may not let intramural sports use their premium facilities, they do not, to our knowledge, actively seek to undermine, belittle, or discourage the efforts of those involved in intramural sports.

Part of the problem with making sense of recreational (amateur) music making in relation to education is that "music" as a school subject is not a direct parallel with most other school subjects. One arguably learns things in school for varied reasons (reflecting differing views on the functions of schooling). Math and language arts, for example, might be conceived primarily in terms of the need for functional numeracy and literacy throughout life. The public can certainly embrace such an idea. School music educators, however, have not enjoyed the perception of a similar "need" because the public does not currently see a need for musicianship throughout life in the way it sees a need for numeracy and literacy (despite the many reported health and wellness benefits of recreational music making). This situation is not helped when school music educators do not conceive of their teaching in terms of a lifelong need for music making.

Compounding the problem is that music educators have never been clear on the possible incommensurability between their espoused and enacted values with respect to music learning. For example, in the first half of the twentieth century, music educators claimed that school music should exist for its "carry over" potential, whereby school music graduates learning music in bands, orchestras, and choirs would become members of community bands, orchestras, and choirs despite complaints that this apparently happened very infrequently. In the second half of the twentieth century the focus shifted in the espoused direction of "aesthetic education"—the long-term value of which has always been rather ambiguous—despite the fact that actual teaching practices remained exactly the same as they were in the early twentieth century.[3]

Music learning and teaching, at least as typically enacted in Canadian and American schools, presents a conundrum with respect to lifelong function and value. To use a sports comparison again: school music, as it is typically offered, is not analogous to physical education, but rather, to varsity sports. School music teaching is more or less homologous to university music teaching, where instruction is predicated on professional performance norms (in the way that varsity sports are predicated on professional sports norms). This is unlikely to change any time soon because the entire school music enterprise in the United States and Canada has been built in this way (e.g., all the spaces, timetabling, the norms and traditions, etc.). It is as if the band, choir, and orchestra are analogous to varsity football, basketball, and volleyball rather than physical education.

While physical education programs no doubt vary considerably from district to district and state to state, the norm in physical education seems to be trending in the direction of teaching students lifelong participation and fitness skills, not teaching students as a form of preparation for varsity sports involvement. A primary difference between music and sports, however, is that, while some sports may be associated with forms of national pride (e.g., American football in the United States, cricket in India and Pakistan), the nature of this association is not cultural on a level comparable to music, which has very deep connections

---

[3] This is something we have written about before (Mantie and Talbot 2015, Talbot and Mantie 2015). The fact that participation in music education remains unchanged is a result of the built-up habits of coloniality (Patel 2016) that perpetuate and reinscribe the power structures of racism and classism in music education. As Chang (2014) writes, "The struggle between restoration and transformation, retrenchment and change, [begins] in culture" (5). Our music education "culture," as Elpus (2015) demonstrates, is primarily taught through the lens of white middle-upper-class music teachers. When 87 percent of the population of music teachers come from this background while the majority of students entering our schools in 2020 are not white, it is not surprising that music education continues to primarily support structures of power that privilege certain backgrounds over others (Bradley 2007, Hess 2015, 2017, Talbot 2018a).

to individual and collective identity. Although some Western classical music proponents might want to make such a claim, there is no universal music equivalent to soccer (or football, as it is known in many countries), a game that transcends national and cultural boundaries. We are not suggesting that collegiate a cappella is the equivalent of soccer's universal appeal. Collegiate a cappella is still culture-bound in the sense that the covering of radio hits reflects a dominant youth culture, one that embodies values that continue to be mostly white and middle class.

We maintain that interdependent agency is a powerful concept with the potential to inform music teaching practices. Interdependent agency is not unproblematic, however. If a premise of education is that it is to serve both the immediate and future needs and interests of students and their communities, then music education must build both dispositions and capacities for lifelong engagement in and with music that must be done within practices that are, by definition, cultural. Thus, while we agree with Regelski that the lack of lifelong participation of music may be attributable to school music not being predicated on "a pluralism of amateurings" (2009, 75), we are not sure how to balance the depth-versus-breadth problem of pluralism in educational settings. That said, it seems imperative that educators who value lifelong musical participation pay greater attention to the ways in which institutionalized music teaching may be inadvertently undermining amateur, recreational music making, through both its enactment of values and its failure to sufficiently develop solo and interdependent musical agency.

7

Future Orientations

"I'm done with extreme music making"

> *The thing about collegiate a cappella is, no one wants the party to end.*
> — Rapkin (2008, 226)

According to Rapkin, graduation represents "the death of one's a cappella career." With journalistic flair, he claims that, for participants, "graduation can be a heartbreaking sucker punch. It's like being torn out of the womb" (270). Indeed, when asked about his future musical involvement, one of our informants, Austin, mentioned the former president of his group: "Now he's graduated and he's kind of sad. He doesn't have his group to go to every Thursday and Sunday night." As our inquiry into this phenomenon unfolded, we became increasingly curious as to how people perceived their participation beyond the college years.

When asked about musical life after college, several of our informants referenced the phenomenon of "post-collegiate a cappella." Feelings were mixed, however. Some eagerly anticipated the opportunity to sustain their a cappella lives. Others were suspect, thinking the idea antithetical to the charm that makes collegiate a cappella special. In response to the thousands of collegiate a cappella singers who don't want their a cappella experience to end, the Contemporary A Cappella League was created in 2007. According to their Facebook page, "CAL is a non-profit organization established to support and grow the adult a cappella community around the globe" (www.facebook.com/pg/acappellaleague/about/). In contrast with church choirs, choral societies, or twentieth-century a cappella singing common to organizations such as the Barbershop Harmony Society or Sweet Adelines International, post-collegiate a cappella notably represents a continuation of the pop cover band style (hence the term "contemporary").

Participants in our research, as gauged by their commitment and passion, prioritized their singing-related activities above many other aspects of their lives during their undergraduate experience. In this chapter we return to our original concern. Given the time-bounded nature of the college years, collegiate a cappella typically has a four-year shelf life. For those who care about lifelong musical involvement, this raises the question, *What happens to musical lives beyond graduation?*

School and Life Connections

A review of the music education literature often leaves one with the impression that "enjoyment" is a dirty word in the academic study of adult music making. This is perhaps understandable when one considers that so much of this research and scholarship in this area is undertaken by those with a vested interest in institutionalized music learning and teaching, not leisure or "well-being." Moreover, because the people conducting the research are, more often than not, products of a system where "expertise" in teaching is the *sine qua non* of professional identity and practice, it is not surprising that activity undertaken by amateurs who dare to engage without the assistance of a "qualified" expert is largely ignored.

None of this is to suggest that research on adult music-making populations does not exist. The (US) National Association for Music Education, for example, has a special research interest group, Adult and Community Music Education, that holds biennial Music and Lifelong Learning symposia. Similarly, the International Society for Music Education has a Community Music Activity commission that holds biennial events dedicated to the research and practice of community (i.e., not school) music. In addition, an entire field of scholarship has emerged around the field of community music, including handbooks, special issues, conferences, and a dedicated international journal on the subject.

There are subtle differences in the foci of lifelong and adult music-making research not to be overlooked. Some commentators (Myers 2008a, Regelski 2007), for example, simply stress the importance of ongoing music making throughout life. Others (Arasi 2006, Chiodo 1997, Coffman 2002a, 2002b, Dabback 2007, Kokotsaki and Hallam 2011, Rohwer and Coffman 2007, Spencer 1996, Vanderark, Newman, and Bell 1983, Wise, Hartmann, and Bradley 1992) point to reported (and self-reported) benefits associated with adult music participation. These studies are complemented by investigations into needs, interests, characteristics, and motivations of adult participants and nonparticipants (Bowen 1995, Busch 2005, Coffin 2005, Coffman 1996, 2008, Faivre-Ransom 2001, Goodrich 2019, Griffith 2006, Hallam et al. 2012, Heintzelman 1988, Larson 1983, Mantie 2012b, Patterson 1985, Pitts and Robinson 2016, Pitts, Robinson, and Goh 2015, Rohwer 2010, Seago 1993, Spell 1989, Spencer 1996, Tatum 1985, Thaller 1999, Tipps 1992, Waggoner 1971), and investigations into "lifespan commitment" (Belz 1994, Chiodo 1997, Coffin 2005, Larson 1983).

Our own interests are closer to research that examines possible connections between school music learning and music making later in life (e.g., Arasi 2006, Bowring 1952, Brown 2012, Burch 2016, Clothier 1967, Falkner 1957, Holmquist 1995, Larson 1983, Lawrence and Dachinger 1967, Lonnberg 1960, Mantie 2012b, 2013, Mantie and Tucker 2008, Moder 2013, Moore, Burland, and Davidson 2003, Mountford 1977, Nazareth 1998, Neal 1949, Ordway 1964, Pitts 2009, 2012a, 2016, 2017, Stein 1970, Thornton 2010, Turton and Durrant 2002, Waggoner 1971, Woody and Parker 2012). In part, our interests are a response to claims and arguments that school music practices in the United States are "failing" and at risk of "irrelevancy" (e.g., Jellison 2000, Myers 2008b, Kratus 2007, Regelski 2005, 2006, Williams 2007, 2011), contributing to what Regelski (2006) dramatically calls school music's "distantiation from society." Our interests are also a response, however, to the general belief, grounded in research (Hallam, Creech, and Varvarigou 2016, Hallam 2015, Creech et al. 2013), that lifelong music making is simply a good and healthy thing for people to do, and it makes little sense for people who have developed sufficient skills for participation to stop doing it. Although we take seriously the charges of commentators (e.g., Myers 1995, 2008b, Jones 2009, Regelski 2005, 2007, D. Williams 2011) that the ensemble instruction model of American school music may not be developing the kinds of musicianship necessary for lifelong participation (see Chapter 6), we are more disturbed by findings (e.g., Arasi 2006, Mantie and Tucker 2008, Woody and Parker 2012) that suggest large ensemble experiences do not provide the kinds of experiences or identities that foster lifelong music making. Collegiate a cappella can obviously not be taken as representative of all possible leisure-time music-making possibilities, and, admittedly, the college years are not far-enough removed from the school music years to provide insights into lifespan engagement (Myers 2008b). We would argue, however, that the perceptions and opinions of collegiate a cappella members do provide important insights that can inform the theory and practice of music learning and teaching because this population chooses to involve themselves in music making when they don't have to, often to the detriment of what should be the reason they have undertaken the expense of attending university (i.e., to attain a degree). The million-dollar question is the extent to which this participation is conceptualized as simply a one-off experience to be reminisced throughout one's life (i.e., "I used to sing in an a cappella group") or as part of a larger vision of leisure-time care and concern.

Beyond Graduation

> For every John Legend, who leaves the UPenn Counterparts and goes on to win Grammy awards, there are thousands of a cappella alums who will never sing again.
>
> — Rapkin (2008, 269)

Both Rapkin (2008) and Duchan (2012a) draw attention to the exceptionality of college as time and place. Rapkin concludes that collegiate a cappella "exists in this incredible space: college. It's the one time in life where everything is momentum… For the same reason one joins a fraternity, or an athletic team, one joins an a cappella group" (270). With allusions to the work of Victor Turner, Duchan similarly writes about students "[passing] through the liminal space and time known as college, a delicate period during which identities are (re)formed on the path from adolescence toward adulthood" (2012, 2–3). One of our research interests was whether our informants considered collegiate a cappella as a college activity akin to Greek life (as alluded to by Rapkin) undertaken during the liminal period of college or whether they considered their participation as part of a life span continuum of musical involvement. To get a better sense of this, we asked participants directly, "What happens to your musical life after you graduate?"

Overall, informants in our study were varied in their responses, exposing differing projections of their imagined futures. Consistent with Rapkin's claims, collegiate a cappella was, for some of our informants, just a thing you did as part of the "college experience." For others, however, collegiate a cappella was part of a larger life trajectory of musical involvement. As Margaret explained, "I don't think I could ever see myself not doing music. I feel like I'll be involved in one way or another throughout my entire life."

It would be unfair to suggest that our informants were so present-focused that they never gave any thought to their imagined musical futures. There were clear differences, however, between those who had ideas about possibilities and those who did not. As Jared admitted, "I have been worried about it; how am I going to sing when I graduate?" More common among those who did not have ideas were indications of avoiding reality (e.g., "I have no godly idea. What outlet can you possibly have?"; "I hope it doesn't stop"; "It's terrible that it's ending and I have no idea what I'm doing. I think singing ends, unfortunately"; "I haven't thought about it. I'm counting on this lasting forever"). Sometimes future considerations were more a matter of ignorance than avoidance, as this exchange with Emily illustrates:

> **Emily:** I don't know. I always worry about that, cause it's kind of like I've built up this much and where do I go next? I've been thinking about trying to join some sort of music ensemble or a band or something that can use my abilities. Because I really don't want to stop after college. 'Cause I don't want it to be the end. It would be awesome if there was some after-college group out there... I remember I was at a wedding and there was an all-male barbershop quartet which was really awesome. But besides that...
>
> **Roger:** So you're not that aware of what musical options exist?
>
> **Emily:** No.
>
> **Roger:** Do you imagine that there are some?
>
> **Emily:** If I don't find any I'll create my own. There are a lot of things I could do, I guess. I could maybe take more lessons.

Of those who had thought about musical life after graduation, there were some who expressed an interest in continuing by taking up accompanying instruments like the piano or guitar following graduation to enjoy more individual forms of music making and those who preferred some form of group music making. There were also those who did not anticipate making music beyond college graduation, either because they felt they wouldn't have time or because they no longer desired to be musically involved. We are hesitant to make quantitative claims about our informants, fearing that speculations on future musical involvement might be inappropriately generalized. Loosely, we would describe our informants as falling into one of five classifications of desire for future musical involvement: *passionate about music, passionate about singing, ambivalent, context-dependent,* and *unlikely*. Such classifications are loose descriptors, but provide additional precision for discussion in the rest of the chapter.

Those within the *passionate about music* category expressed a variety of imagined futures, ranging from the definite (e.g., "I think I'll take up the piano again and learn covers of songs and sing them at open mic nights"; "I don't have my guitar here, but when I go home I'll do that"; "I still have a guitar and I'll always play that"; "I'm going to pursue my own songwriting career"; "I don't know how much I want to admit this, but I like to write songs sometimes") to the more speculative (e.g., "I've let piano slide the past few years. I might try to pick that up again"; "Music in my future will change forms. I'll probably start recording my own stuff"; "I can imagine arranging things; when I come home from work I'll need to do something"), to the unknown (e.g., "music has always been such a big part of my life; I can't imagine living without music"; "I'd like to pursue my own songwriting career, but I'm torn. Music has been an escape, a hobby. If it becomes a business, what else could I turn to?"). For this group of informants, what appeared to matter most was being involved in music in some way. References to piano and guitar, as well as songwriting, arranging, and recording, would seem to suggest a more individualized or personal approach to musical involvement not dependent on coordination with other people.

Those we classified as *passionate about singing* were, in our estimation, among the most emphatic about their desire for future musical involvement. We heard a few responses that were equivocal about their anticipated musical futures (e.g., "Whenever I go home I sing in my family's church choir. If I could find a good choir, I'd do that"; "I'm likely going to keep up with singing on a religious level"), but more common were expressions that left little doubt that their collegiate a cappella experience was not simply a one-off activity as part of the college experience (e.g., "I can't live without singing; even if I don't join an a cappella group I'll take singing lessons"; "I think I would be unhappy if I didn't keep singing"; "I'm married to music; it's not going away. I can't imagine not singing. I will always be a part of something, either by starting my own community service group or joining a barbershop quartet—whatever—I will be singing"). Several of our informants mentioned post-collegiate a cappella (e.g., "I have friends who are trolling for post-collegiate a cappella"; "I'll do post-collegiate a cappella; I don't think I could ever see myself not doing music"). Miranda, the music director of an all-female group, told us she was looking forward to the opportunity of singing without the leadership responsibilities: "As music director I don't sing as much by myself. I look forward to getting back to that. Institutionalized singing has been such a large part of my life since I was eight." Notably, the informants in this category all made reference to music making as a group activity. What appeared to matter most was not just singing but singing *with others*.

Some informants seem best described as *ambivalent* based on responses that suggest that future musical involvement would likely depend on opportunities and circumstances (e.g., "I hope I'll be involved, but I don't know how much that will be possible. I've let piano slide the past few years. I might try to pick that up again"; "being a teacher I might not have the time"; "I don't think I'll have the opportunity to sing or make music but I'd definitely consider it. I'd like to be in a community choir"). This group of informants might be described as "realists" to the extent their responses demonstrate an awareness of what employed adult life might be like. Their responses suggest an enjoyment of music making, but an enjoyment subject to time and effort constraints. Collegiate a cappella participation for those in this category is arguably viewed as more than just a college activity. Overall, their interviews evinced a definite love for music, but a love that might not translate into the kind of commitment necessary to make recreational music making part of their future lifestyle.

The *context-dependent* category describes those informants for whom the possibility of future musical participation would be less a matter of desire or convenience of opportunity, and more a matter of a good "fit." This group is significant for what it reveals about the relationship between musical desire and musical practice, especially insofar as we noted a division between those who expressed a preference for continuing with some form of a cappella singing (i.e., post-collegiate a cappella), sustaining what they were currently doing, and those who expressed a disinterest in future a cappella singing.

Sometimes, interest in post-collegiate a cappella was subject to the constraints of imagined futures, as in these two examples:

> I hope it doesn't stop. I've considered post. In college I was always hoping to find people who would continue to make music with me for the rest of our lives. (Anika)

* * *

> In all likelihood, I probably won't have time to join an a cappella group after I graduate. But I still have a guitar, and I would definitely play that—so musically I'd stay involved. But like I said, I would love to get an a cappella group together, but it would have to be super casual. (Craig)

Craig's reference to "super casual" introduces a tension we discerned in several interviews, one that speaks in some ways to the issue of "how good is good enough" we discussed in Chapter 2. On the one hand, several informants anticipated they would not be able to justify the same level of time and energy commitment to their singing in the future as they currently devote. On the other hand, some informants expressed concerns that without a high level of commitment, the experience might not be sufficiently rewarding or enjoyable. Leslie, for example, in response to a question about post-collegiate a cappella, replied, "I've heard mixed things. They turn more into social groups. Here at college we are so driven; we are pretty disciplined. I'd be hesitant to join a group after college." Similarly, Beth explained, "I want to do something musical, but I really do think that unless you're in one of those exceptional situations where you find a not-hokey recreational group or a wildly successful professional group, it's really not a plausible thing." For Beth, in other words, collegiate a cappella can seem "hokey" when done recreationally. However, when taken to the level of professional standards (e.g., Pentatonix), a cappella can apparently transcend the perception or feeling of hokiness—but building toward such a level would likely require a level of commitment not viewed as realistic for recreational participation.

The *unlikely* category also provides an interesting case for those concerned about lifelong music making, insofar as it highlights the risks that occur when the demands of the activity exceed what is considered sustainable over a lifetime. The commitment in many performance-intensive groups often robs people of their ability to control their time, leading Rapkin to wonder, "When is it all too much?" (2008, 199). Although a minority, several informants did respond to our question about future music making with comments such as, "I need a break. I think I'm done. Singing once I have a job, I don't find that appealing"; "I've had my good run. I'm done with music. There are other things I want to try"; and our personal favorite, "I'm done with extreme music making"—a phrase that underscores how, at least in some groups, collegiate a cappella is not undertaken as a recreational activity akin to intramural sports, but a serious, high-stakes endeavor similar to NCAA Tier I sports.

* * *

Rapkin compares collegiate a cappella alumni reunions (and, by extension, post-collegiate a cappella) to a pitiful bit of nostalgia comparable to Will Ferrell starting a fraternity for adults in the 2003 Hollywood comedy *Old School*. "Some memories," he suggests, "are better left in the past" (2008, 271). Along similar lines, many of our informants expressed negative opinions about post-collegiate a cappella, with most comments reflecting the general view that, similar to Greek life, collegiate a cappella is defined not so much by its singing, but by a kind of sociality tied to time and place (e.g., "a cappella loses its charm after college; those people didn't really move on"; "I would never do post-collegiate a cappella. There's a time for a cappella. Post—it's not the same atmosphere"; "I'll probably do musical theatre. I would never do post-collegiate a cappella.

I wouldn't grow up!"; "You should have your time and then you should move on"). There is arguably nothing wrong with time-bound practices. One does not typically remain a high school student for life, for example. The liminal nature of collegiate a cappella would seem to present an interesting case for those concerned about lifelong music making, however.

What Have We Learned?

> A cappella is a choice college students make, a choice to stand up and sing, to perform, to compete, to serenade, to profit, to hide, to seek truth, to find answers, and to commemorate.
>
> — Rapkin (2008, 14)

In Chapter 1 we acknowledged that not all high school graduates attend university and that to study the activities of collegiate a cappella participants is to study a population that is, by definition, privileged in various ways and certainly not demographically representative of the general population. Nevertheless, 60–70 percent of high school graduates do attend university, and, while the percentage of students who participate in collegiate a cappella is very small, collegiate a cappella still involves thousands of people who choose to spend their discretionary time singing in a student-run group rather than doing other things while at university. Scholars in the sociology of leisure often argue that children have *play*, not *recreation*—a distinction grounded in a work-leisure dichotomy (i.e., children do not have recreation because they do not "work" for a living). By extension, the nonacademic college activities of university students can be thought to exist in something of a *quasi*-recreational space because students are studying, not "working." Just as childhood is time-bound, so too is the typical four-year undergraduate degree. University recreational (or leisure) activities occur within a context understood as temporary—a stage of life suspended from what came before (childhood) and what will come after (the world of "work"). This stage is, in this sense, liminal, but liminal not just as an "in between" period but as one that for many people is profoundly transformational. For many students, the university years are usually the first opportunity for significant decision-making while no longer under direct parental care and exert a tremendous influence over the values that help to determine the kinds of people they become. Understanding the ways in which university students conceive of their volitional choices and activities outside of their professionally oriented (or at least, work-oriented) studies is of great importance to those of us who care about such things as individual and collective well-being beyond what people do for a living.

When one looks beneath the cover song veneer, it turns out that there is a lot more going on in collegiate a cappella than at first meets the eye (and ear). The motivations of participants, for example, are diverse. Some students are clearly attracted to the novelty and (un)cool factor of singing in an a cappella group as part of their college experience with the expectation of looking back nostalgically in their imagined futures. Others just really need to sing, and collegiate a cappella is a fun and convenient outlet for their musical passions. What was encouraging, from the perspective of researchers wanting to understand how participants conceived of their singing in the broader context of their lives, were the responses that suggested a decided intentionality in terms of singing as crucial for personal well-being (i.e., creating balance against the rigors of academic life). These responses, however, were offset by the number of people who felt that this balance was really only necessary during the university years and that, inexplicably, they doubted they would have the time or inclination for such activity postgraduation.

Our informants' views on the importance of being good did vary somewhat, but our unsurprising conclusion, based on all the interviews and observations we conducted, is that most people want to be good, but not at the expense of happiness. There is a rationalizing cost-benefit analysis at work, and while the calculation may vary slightly from person to person, it was fascinating how much the calculation coalesced around a similar amount of time and effort. The ICCAs provided a convenient goal and motivator for some groups, but for others the competitive aspect of the ICCAs actually detracted by shifting the locus of enjoyment from singing to winning. Contrary to the "excellence" paradigm central to university music instruction (which very often makes its way into school music instruction as well), our informants expressed a "threshold" paradigm: they didn't need to be the best—they needed to be *good enough*. This did not mean a lack of effort or desire, but rather, attaining a level of performance that felt rewarding and commensurate with the amount of time and effort put forth.

One is left, then, wondering about what all this might mean for those who care about sociocultural issues and music making throughout the life span. To the extent that school music programs are able to develop forms of musical agency that enable people to participate in music making throughout the life span, great; our informants, to the extent their abilities are attributable to school (rather than out-of-school) learning, are clear examples of successful teaching. At the same time, many of them also expressed concerns that they wished they had a better understanding of "how music worked"—something they felt they did not learn from their school music programs.

Beyond the self-reported motivations, justifications, and lifestyle conceptualizations of our informants, we were struck by how collegiate a cappella participates in the perpetuation of various forms of inequality. The whiteness and upper-middle-class nature of collegiate a cappella is hardly surprising, given its Ivy League origins. That said, one might have expected to see more instances of resistance or at least self-reflexiveness, if only on a modest scale. Instead, we are left with the conclusion that, as a socio-musical practice, collegiate a cappella will continue to enact, privilege, and reproduce values that equate "difference" with personality or people who are pursuing a different academic major. The privileging of heteronormativity is similarly problematic, although not surprising, given the close historical associations with Greek life and its fraternities and sororities—institutions that are known for their performance and perpetuation of heteronormative values. The heteronormativity of collegiate a cappella is troubling, of course, especially for those outside the norms, but the ways in which heteronormativity translates into male advantage in the structure of participation in a cappella is particularly disturbing to us. We did encounter a few females frustrated by gender inequality in collegiate a cappella, but these were the exception and not the rule. For the most part, participants couldn't quite put their finger on the problem with this hierarchy and seemed to just accept gender inequality as "the way of the world."

Finally, we are left wondering what these various forms of inequality we witnessed might mean for those involved with the teaching enterprise. Do school choral programs reflect these same values? As discussed in Chapters 3 and 4, there is plenty of scholarship to suggest male advantage in singing is not limited to collegiate a cappella and that it is firmly entrenched in the structures of participation in our schools. Taking into consideration, then, the obvious displays of male privileging in collegiate a cappella perpetuated through the audition process, the gendered voicing, the repertoire choices, and costuming, what parallels can current music teachers make about their own programs? What changes to these structures of participation might teachers begin to make to dismantle forms of patriarchal oppression found within school music singing programs?

Collegiate a cappella practices are "performative" to the extent they (re)iterate norms of who males and females are and "should be" both in music education and in American society at large. As we learned from Josh's and Alex's stories in Chapter 4, the gender- and hetero-normativity inherent in collegiate a cappella is troubling. What considerations might school music teachers make to support sexual- and gender-diverse individuals in their classrooms? How might the gendered nature of voice classification and repertoire influence student experiences? How do recruitment, marketing, and rehearsal practices in school music programs reinscribe gender- and hetero-normativity?

8

Beyond Graduation

"My mom looked at me and said, 'You need to sing!'"

As we neared the completion of what we thought was the first draft of the manuscript, we reflected on the time period that elapsed since we began our initial data collection back in 2011. We began to wonder about the people with whom we interacted over the years. Where are they now? What are their memories and their current thoughts about their time with their a cappella group? Are they still musically active? We realized we needed to do some follow-up interviews.

Having been at Gettysburg College for over ten years, Brent had closer relationships and contact with the alumni members of Gettysburg's a cappella groups. In addition, the prominence of the college's music school within a relatively small liberal arts college meant the a cappella groups had a higher percentage of music majors in them than is common on most campuses (where music majors are rare)—meaning that Brent, as a music faculty member, knew more students in the campus's a cappella groups than a typical music professor. Although his original faculty involvement was with the campus's all-male ensemble, he came to know members in the campus's other groups as well. On the basis of convenience and personal knowledge about individual backgrounds that would assist our research, Brent reached out to five Gettysburg alumni who participated in a cappella, one of whom he had interviewed in 2014, for "postscript" interviews.

Roger's situation was different. With the exception of "Michelle," whom he had met while serving as a faculty adviser for jazz combo groups at Boston University, he did not have any "inside" contacts or close relationships with the people he originally interviewed. Thanks to social media and the internet, however, he reconnected with six of his original informants from 2011–2013 in order to conduct postscript interviews. These six (three male, three female) represented a convenience sample, albeit one generated with some purposeful stratification (e.g., one female co-ed, one male co-ed, etc.). Surprisingly, everyone contacted agreed to do a follow-up interview. This was rather remarkable (and telling), in that, with the exception of Michelle, informants had only interacted with Roger one time many years in the past. Combined, our postscript interviewees ranged in age from approximately twenty-two to thirty. They were drawn from the US northeast, where all of them continue to reside (although a few had lived elsewhere for brief periods).

As we have discussed throughout this book, our primary data collection occurred at what might be described in hindsight as collegiate a cappella's apex of popularity in American culture. Our motivations at the time were not based on opportunism, but rather, our interest in lifelong musical participation and its possible connections with music learning, especially music learning in and through schooling. Nevertheless, the topical aspects of collegiate a cappella, arguably reaching their zenith shortly after the release of the first *Pitch Perfect* movie, provided an unforeseen "value-added" to our project.

At the time of this writing, *Pitch Perfect 3* (released 2017) has earned $185 million, enough to claim the title of the second-highest grossing musical comedy to date (behind only *Pitch Perfect 2* at $287 million). One might interpret this as indicative of sustained interest in collegiate a cappella. Indeed, shows like *The Voice* or *America's Got Talent*, which frequently feature singing acts, might suggest that the American public is still enraptured by singing entertainment. Shows like *Glee* and *The Sing-Off*, however, are no longer on the air, and, as one of our postscript interviewees told us, a cappella is no longer the campus-wide sensation it used to be. All-male groups that used to sell out 1000-seat (and even 4000-seat) auditoriums, for example, are apparently now struggling to draw a hundred people. Despite the popularity of *Pitch Perfect 3*, in other words, many other measures seem to suggest the shine of group singing as pop culture phenomenon has begun to fade. Intriguingly, however, it would appear that the practice of collegiate a cappella is as strong as ever, with competition at auditions fierce and new college groups (and post-collegiate groups) continuing to emerge. According to our postscript interviewees and a cursory examination of recent YouTube performances, the talent level in collegiate a cappella groups is as good as (or better than) it has ever been. As one interviewee optimistically put it, for today's participants, "the disappearance of the hype is almost a weight off their shoulders."

Where Are They Now?

One recalls that our original pool of informants included some students at public institutions, but the overwhelming majority of them attended private colleges and universities, including several schools generally considered "elite." Our sample, in other words, was hardly representative of society at large. Nevertheless, by many common measures of life "success," our postscript interviewees have done well. Two went into law (one currently at an Ivy League law school, the other beginning a job in Manhattan at a major law firm), one followed their degree path and is employed as an engineer, one works as an admissions director at a prestigious preparatory school, one works for a major nonprofit in a health-related field, three work in research and development-related fields, and one works in retail and gigs as a freelance musician. The remaining two, following their career paths in music education, now work as elementary music teachers. As might be predicted for those in the twenty-two to thirty age range, about half were married or in relationships; none had children. None expressed to us any dissatisfaction about their lives three to eight years beyond graduation. From what we could glean, they appeared generally happy, healthy, and positive.

Legacy of Participation

All of our postscript interviewees spoke glowingly about their time in collegiate a cappella. Their opinions about their experiences were as positive as they were during their undergraduate years. They said things like "wildly critical to who I am," "I wouldn't have made it through college without music," and "wish I could do it again now." Although this might have been expected on one level—in that self-selection would predict a positive response from those who elected to participate for multiple years in such a high-intensity activity—we were nonetheless surprised that not one interviewee expressed anything less than glowing nostalgia.

One of our lines of questioning for our postscript interviewees explored what they considered to be some of the longer-term impacts (i.e., the legacy) of their collegiate a cappella involvement. We asked interviewees to name specific skills they felt they may have developed or acquired through a cappella participation. Most pointed to interpersonal skills, mentioning they felt more comfortable with being in groups with people of varying interests. They spoke about how their involvement gave them the confidence to pitch ideas, sell products, and speak comfortably to people both in small and large groups. As one interviewee said, "I think the amount of personal interaction I have on a daily basis with my job, a lot of public speaking, and being comfortable in front of an audience is definitely something that is attributable to my time in a cappella. I think that is a big part of why I have become decent at what I do." As another informant who now works in a law firm and engages with over 150 summer associates explained, "We were all very different people—a bunch of weirdos. A cappella gave me the skills to get along with everyone even when I didn't know them well or even like some of them." The ability to work as a team also came up consistently in the interviews. One interviewee stated that collegiate a cappella was what "got him to Apple." Other interviewees shared stories of major corporate deadlines that needed to be met and paralleled these experiences to the shared sense of ownership and responsibility necessary to complete the job after hitting creative walls during their a cappella days.

Concrete skill development (beyond musical skills) is no doubt an added ancillary benefit of collegiate a cappella. This pales, however, in comparison with the value of the social and cultural capital accrued. Responses from our postscript interviewees very much reinforce what we discussed in Chapter 5. Many interviewees indicated they listed their involvement and leadership roles in a cappella on their résumés and that it was frequently discussed during interviews. One, who now works at a Fortune 500 company, was explicit about the matter: "a cappella is why I have gotten my jobs." (It just so happens that one of the top executives at his current employer is an alumnus of the same a cappella group.) Another interviewee echoed this sentiment, stating, "I got my job because of a connection to someone in the a cappella world." One interviewee shared that an interview committee saw an online video of her singing, while another stated how he mentioned being the treasurer of his a cappella group to an interview committee "to show leadership skills and to indicate experience working with bureaucracy."

Nate reported that a cappella is not usually a topic that is directly brought up in interviews but is instead explored through conversations about how he manages free time:

> I'm always asked, "So what do you for fun?" A good answer I always say is, "Well, I was president of my a cappella my senior year and I loved doing it." And people would more often than not be a little bit amazed by that—or I will often find people saying, "Oh, I was in a group as well" or "Cool! You got to do all those things they did in *Pitch Perfect* and Pentatonix."

Nate went on to explain that, in his current role as an admissions director, he uses his involvement with collegiate a cappella groups to appear more relatable to prospective students and their families. "During interviews students and their families see my group's poster on my wall and ask about it. I proudly put it there to let people know I did something for fun that was expressive."

As one of our interviewees pointed out to us, "Everyone has music in some way or other." Thus, it is not necessarily that surprising that a cappella involvement serves as a conversation starter. It is the depth of experience, however, that helps to set collegiate a cappella alumni apart. Many of those interviewed discussed the instant bonds that occurred among colleagues and coworkers who shared their experiences and associations with singing in collegiate a cappella groups. One interviewee, for example said, "A receptionist in my office was in a group in college, and so we have that weird unique bond with one another." Another recounted how his best friend in law school just happened to be an alumnus of a well-known a cappella group at a neighboring school.

The instant relationships formed with new colleagues and coworkers are important. So too, however, are the lasting friendships that result from four years of shared undergraduate experiences. Distance is no longer the barrier it might have been twenty to thirty years ago due to social media and the internet. A couple of our postscript interviewees reported not being overly close with former group members, but all the rest shared stories of ongoing friendships. Barry, for example, mentioned that his former a cappella group members are "still his closest friends," a sentiment echoed by Jack, who talked about getting together with Rob every couple of months to play D&D (Dungeons & Dragons). "We still make a point to stay close. He is still to this day one of my favorite people on this earth. I love that man to death." Several other interviewees reported attending the weddings of former group members (with two serving as bridesmaids). Others mentioned regularly attending alumni shows or getting together during the holidays (when members were more likely to be in the same city).

Wokeness?

The on-demand world of television streaming services now makes it possible to binge-watch once popular American shows like Seinfeld and Friends. While certain anachronisms, such as fashion trends or large home telephones with aerials, help to date such shows, it is the nature of the comedy itself that serves as a reminder how social values change and that what might have been thought humorous at one time is considered politically incorrect at another. *Seinfeld* and *Friends*, for example, date from the 1990s. It is perhaps not that surprising for societal values around gender and sexuality to have evolved since that time. *Glee*, however, dates only from 2009. While considered by some as quite progressive in addressing such issues as teen pregnancy and gay/lesbian relationships, a retrospective viewing in 2020 reveals ongoing stereotypes of positioning singing as "gay" (e.g., season one).

The pace of change in sociocultural values is often slow but is occasionally accelerated by significant events. Most obvious in this regard is #MeToo, which has arguably shifted conversations around gender and sexuality in ways that other movements have not. With respect to collegiate a cappella, one is beginning to see shifts in perceptions and values. For example, 2019 marked the tenth anniversary of a celebrated all-male a cappella concert entitled "Men Being Manly." The advertising in 2019, however, exhibited a marked change from earlier years:

> In addition to being a celebration of all-male a cappella, we're partnering this year with 16,000 Strong @ BU (a Boston University student-run campaign created to foster a movement against sexual assault and violence) to redefine what it means to be Men Being Manly—proceeds will be donated to them!

To take another example, the long-standing all-male ensemble at Gettysburg College instituted a change in its branding in 2019. Whereas it historically billed itself as the campus's "premiere all-male a cappella group," it now calls itself "the premiere lower-voiced a cappella group." Perhaps most telling in this regard is a response from one of our postscript interviewees, a former music director for a high-profile all-male group, who noted how "the all-male anything has played itself out; it almost feels inappropriate."

Gender and Sexuality

One of our curiosities with our postscript interviews was with views on gender and sexuality. Only a handful of our original set of interviews demonstrated (or at least shared with us) an awareness of gender and sexual inequality in the collegiate a cappella world. Those interviews, it should be added, were exclusively with members of all-female groups. Males, and female members in co-ed groups, did not mention anything substantial about gender and sexual inequality in their original interviews. Were our informants now more aware of possible gender and sexual inequality that existed when they were undergraduates? Did they have opinions on such matters now?

In most cases, the answer to the first question was "no." Five male interviewees, for example, admitted they had never thought about gender inequality in a cappella until we asked about it in the postscript interview. (One claimed that gender wasn't an issue at his university.) Michelle, a former member of a co-ed group, confessed that no one ever brought up gender during her time in the group—although she predicted that the "next generation" of a cappella was going to change in response to changes in gender identities in society. Leslie, a former all-female group member, reiterated the same keen insights, concerns, and frustrations she had expressed six years earlier—which was not only fascinating in that she had not been prompted or cued in any way prior to our query but also intriguing in that her views had not seemingly changed in the intervening years.

Answers to the second question proved more interesting, in that the postscript interviewees—several years older and with the benefit of hindsight—were able to offer perspectives and opinions that provided additional nuance to understandings of gender and inequality in the a cappella world. Most overt in this regard was an acknowledgment of the masculinist nature of all-male groups at the time, which was described by two male interviewees as "fratty" and "douchey frat-bro."[1] As Barry explained about his group's identity, "the machismo and misogyny is what they were about"—although he also qualified this by noting that being "super talented" was what justified the persona and distinguished it from being unacceptable in the way that frat-like behavior might be in other contexts. They were, he said, "a fraternity that just happened to sing," by which he did not mean the negative clichéd connotations of Greek life fraternities, but rather, the positive aspects of friendship and brotherhood.

Derek offered us a perspective that challenges straightforward assumptions about male hegemony in society. He noted that, for many males at the time he was growing up, singing in the K-12 years was not accepted or acceptable. As some of the "missing males" research discussed in Chapter 4 has suggested, singing in schools was (and often still is) perceived as effeminate or "gay," leading to much ostracization. Derek loved music but did not feel safe singing in elementary school. He took up the clarinet instead. By high school he had enrolled in choir, but still he felt a sense of isolation. It should not necessarily come as a surprise, then, that males in collegiate a cappella—especially those in all-male groups at the time of our data collection—took up a "fratty" persona that flaunted hypermasculinity. For Derek, all-male collegiate a cappella groups represented a kind of vindication: "Males who finally can sing and it's an attractive attribute!" Barry had an even more perspicacious take on the identity and persona of all-male groups: "the social aspect coupled with musicality allows the guys to be what society doesn't want them to be."

---

[1] Rapkin noted that Masi Oka, an actor on NBC's television show *Heroes*, who was the music director for Brown University's all-male group, The Bear Necessities, described his group as a geeky frat: "It was brothership" (2008, 11).

Societal perceptions of male singing are extraordinarily complex, of course. If there is a lesson to be learned here, it is that, as we discussed in Chapter 4, singing practices participate in the performativity of gender and sexuality in ways that construct and reinscribe power relations and hierarchies. For those who care about equity and the right of all people to lead meaningful lives, the importance of "safe spaces" as a strategy to resist inequalities cannot be emphasized enough. The hypermasculinity of all-male collegiate a cappella can be viewed as a compensatory response to the threat to masculinity posed by many school singing settings. At the same time, the hypermasculinity of all-male a cappella groups can create its own hostile environment. Indeed, we heard one story of a gay male who felt so uncomfortable that he left an all-male group for a co-ed group:

> I heard that Alex left the group because he didn't feel welcome—that it was like too hyper-masculine an environment for him. I didn't know he felt that way. I actually felt the group dynamic was quite good. I'm sorry and ashamed that this was how he felt about his experience. I don't know, maybe it got worse after I graduated… (Jack)

Josh expressed how he felt during his first year: "I would have been uncomfortable at an audition for [group name] because the all-male a cappella group was just too 'bro-y' for lack of a better term." He went on to explain, "I was more attracted to the co-ed group because the all-male one was too much like a fraternity for me. And that's not a safe space for gay people like me or even effeminate straight people." Josh's comments here, we would argue, are guilty of essentialist assumptions about the relationship between gay males and masculinity that are dismissive of the spectrum of possibilities and preferences of gay males. For example, Barry, who is also gay, very much embraced the hypermasculine identity of his all-male group. Josh's point, however, is well-taken: there are always winners and losers in unsafe environments (which, for the winners, is exactly the point). It is a zero-sum game.

This discussion about safe spaces and masculinity leaves one in the all-too-familiar place of privileging the lives of males over the lives of females (see O'Toole 2000). To a large extent, this reflects our limitations as scholars and researchers. For us, the performative constructions of femininity, beyond overt and obvious gendered inequalities, feel exceptionally complex, a point driven home in our postscript interview with Julie, a former all-female group member. Julie was direct and forthright in her appraisals of gender and inequality in collegiate a cappella. For her, the hypermasculinity of male singers reflected a form of self-selection: "The guys who are brave enough to sing are the ones good enough or confident enough." She explained that males in a cappella had to continue enacting fraternity and hypermasculinity: "Otherwise you are just guys singing show tunes." By contrast, Julie lamented what she perceived as the phenomenon where "every girl thinks they can sing," something she felt actually undermined female solidarity. As noted in Chapter 3, Julie was originally reticent about joining an all-female group. In our postscript interview she reminisced about those feelings, reiterating how transformational her all-female singing experience was in helping teach her to be around females. She shared with Roger that she had recently been reading psychology-related books on female friendships. These books had led her to question many social norms and values related to femininity and female-on-female competition. "It's just not true," she relayed. Paraphrasing a book she was currently reading, she posed the question, "Who told us that and why did we believe it?" She believed that part of the solution to better gender equality, both in collegiate a cappella (and in society), was for females to "stop being mean to each other."

The final interviews of current a cappella participants for this project occurred in spring of 2019. Those two interviews (i.e., original informant interviews with current participants, not postscript interviews) hardly provide a sufficient sample size to make bold generalizations, but it is still worth noting that the responses to our gender and sexuality-related questions in 2019 were very different from the interviews we conducted in the 2011–2016 time period—almost to the extent our originally worded questions (which we still used) felt awkward or strange to the informants. The consensus among our postscript interviewees was a cautious optimism about reduced gender inequality in collegiate a cappella (mixed, in one case, with a sense of loss). Julie, for example, asserted that "female friendships are making a comeback" in society, which will inevitably help to create a better climate for collegiate a cappella. Consistent with Michelle's prediction that the next generation was going to change in response to societal norms around gender, Barry—who had recently attended a retreat with the current members of his all-male group—reported, "The current guys are much more sensitive and expressive." With a whiff of nostalgia about his group's former bravado, however, he added that the members today are "so thoughtful"; the current group, he opined, "has lost its swag."

Diversity: Race and Class

> I was so sad when Jamal [a student of color] left the group because I love him. He told us, "I don't feel welcome here; it sucks," but framed it in a way that was more, "I wanted to make music and this group feels like it's more of a social group than

> a music group." But I knew what he meant. He really didn't feel like he belonged, that he had a place. And that's sad. It's very sad. It's interesting because it certainly wasn't a conscious effort on the part of us to be exclusively a white-male focused group. But I think in many ways our attitude and the way we presented ourselves made it unapproachable to those who don't fit that category. (Jack)

We have repeatedly noted in this book how collegiate a cappella's middle- to upper-class whiteness is attributable, in part, to its historical origins with Ivy League schools and the exclusivity of Greek life fraternities. We have also mentioned Winstead's (2013) historical examination of college singing, which, among other things, documents the prevalent and high-level singing activities at historically black colleges and universities (HBCUs). Given the substantial social and cultural capital accrued through contemporary collegiate a cappella participation, however, the perpetuation of whiteness and privilege represents a problem for those who care about issues of access, inclusion, and diversity. We were, therefore, curious to see if our postscript interviewees had any current thoughts on the ongoing lack of diversity of both race and class in the a cappella world.

A conclusion that stands out for us is that, while our postscript interviewees were quite thoughtful and sensitive in their responses, many continued to rationalize the existence of the lack of diversity. For example, Julie drew attention to a cappella's origins in the Ivy Leagues and how self-selection helped to explain the overwhelming whiteness in collegiate a cappella. "People stick with what they know," she pointed out. These sentiments connect to the story of Jamal from above, who left the group because—though he loved singing cover songs for large adoring audiences—he always felt like an outsider in the group. As Jack (a cis-gender white male) points out in the retelling of this experience, "it certainly wasn't a conscious effort on the part of us to be exclusively a white-male focused group." Now pursuing a law degree focused on advocacy for minority groups, Jack offered some recognition of the role white privilege and unconscious bias contributed to Jamal's feelings of isolation when he said, "But I think in many ways our attitude and the way we presented ourselves made it unapproachable to those who don't fit that category."

There were also a few questionable assumptions related to race and diversity in the interviews. One postscript interviewee, for example, claimed his university was quite diverse. Current statistics on undergraduate enrollment at his former university's website lists 5.4 percent of the student body as Black/African American and 12.2 percent Hispanic/Latino, which is admittedly more diverse than several other universities in the area, but is nonetheless far from what might qualify as diverse based on the population at large.[2] Another interviewee thought the lack of diversity in the local collegiate a cappella scene simply reflected Boston being a predominantly white city. In fact, Boston's population is currently only about 53 percent white (although the city's public spaces admittedly do tend to present as mostly white).

While none of the postscript interviewees disputed the lack of diversity in collegiate a cappella, this lack was accepted as to be expected, rather than being regarded as a problem necessarily in need of addressing. One outlier in this regard was Leslie, who shared that her a cappella group was very "social justicey" and regularly discussed the problem of diversity during her years in the group. They would, she said, talk about ways to make their group more inclusive. Upon reflection, she confessed that, despite good intentions, their group's activities were actually "not helpful or conducive to encouraging diversity"—something perhaps not that surprising at an elite private liberal arts college comprising a predominantly white and upper-class student body. She conveyed that she continues to think about the kinds of invisible barriers in society that mitigate broader participation by all its members but is unsure how to help change the conditions that create such barriers.

Although Derek admitted that his group did not necessarily discuss diversity at the time, he mentioned that he has come to see the lack of diversity in the collegiate a cappella world as a problem. He described the ICCAs, for example, as "very culty" (by which he meant clique-like). He also speculated that "it's not necessarily attractive to lower-income populations." Derek's appraisal is, in fact, supported by research (e.g., Carlsson, Daruvala, and Johansson-Stenman 2005, Hryshko, Luengo-Prado, and Sørensen 2011, Brown and Pol 2015) that suggests lower-income parents tend to be less risk-averse, favoring "practical" degree programs over liberal arts education. The perception of collegiate a cappella as a frivolous, time-wasting activity is indeed a likely factor that helps to explain the lack of diversity—the irony being that lower socioeconomic-status students end up losing out on the very advantageous social and cultural capital accrued through a cappella participation (i.e., "a cappella is why I have gotten my jobs").

We would argue that the lack of diversity in collegiate a cappella is a regrettable but intractable problem insofar as there are few mechanisms for corrective action beyond individual or group-level commitments to the importance of diversity—and even then, as Leslie's example shows, the obstacles can feel insurmountable.

---

[2] Recent reports from The US Census Bureau project that, by the middle of 2020, nonwhites will account for the majority of the nation's 74 million children. www.pbs.org/newshour/nation/children-of-color-projected-to-be-majority-of-u-s-youth-this-year, accessed January 19, 2020.

The many contributing factors that work against access and inclusion are the very structural issues that prop up privilege and the advantage of whiteness. For example, while Barry observed how his group's alumni has broadened beyond its traditional "New Jersey north" geographic area to include international students from places like Germany and Australia, he also drew attention to how the high-functioning school music programs (in the United States) that develop the kinds of skills and awareness that increase the chances of being accepted into collegiate a cappella groups tend to be concentrated in predominantly white communities. At the opposite end of the spectrum, professional role-model groups perpetuate an image of whiteness, as Josh pointed out for us: "I mean even with professional a cappella groups like Cantus, Straight No Chaser, and Chanticleer there is still something so blue-blooded and blazer about it." Put differently, the structural forces often make it seem as though there is nothing that can be done. At a minimum, one hopes that educators everywhere can continue to stress the importance of equity and diversity in society. Building stronger awareness of how unconscious bias operates and the ways educators contribute to systems of advantage, for example, is but one strategy that may help ensure whiteness and privilege are not just overlooked or ignored but disrupted and addressed.

Thoughts on Leisure-Time Music Making

> Reflecting on it now, I think the experience is and should be less about the quality of your performance and more about the quality of the time you spend together. It's a way to have fun doing something and to share that together. Nobody cares if the group is perfectly in tune on the power ballad they sing on the end of their show. What you really care about is being together. So *that's* what I would encourage to undergrad students who are considering joining a cappella. Definitely do it and make the group your own and make sure you are doing it to have fun and to make friends. (Jack)

If there is one thing we hope to have made clear in this book, it is that the social and the musical are more like two sides of a coin than two separate modes of experience. We would argue, based on our research, that the driving force for participants (social and musical) is in constant flux, both in the moment and over time. Our original informants were clear that without the music, there would be little to hold people together, but, as Michelle so perceptibly put it in our postscript interview, "If it's not social, it's not musical." In one sense this helps to explain some of the lack of diversity found in so many a cappella groups. The need for social cohesion trumps considerations of musical talent (or musical talent is defined along social lines), leading most groups to "pick their friends" in ways that ensure a certain kind of homogeneity. Although this might be viewed in a negative light in terms of affirmative action on diversity and inclusion, it also reflects that, when it comes to volitional involvement in leisure activities, people desire experiences they anticipate as positive and rewarding. Social dysfunction undermines the *raison d'être* of collegiate a cappella. This is in no way to suggest that diversity and inclusion result in or contribute to social dysfunction, but it hopefully does make clear that participants believe they are acting rationally and in the best interests of current members when they select people they perceive as the best "fit."[3] One line of questioning for the postscript interviewees explored their reflections on music-making experiences during their undergraduate years and their thoughts on possible connections to what we described in Chapter 6 as "musical agency." As we discuss in further detail below, their responses reveal greater agreement than we found in our original interviews. We originally found a range of opinions in response to the question, *How important is it to be good?*, with many informants stressing that, within reason, excellence motivated by competition was central to their participation. Almost all postscript interviewees admitted, however, that if they were to do it over again, they might take a more relaxed approach to their music making.

Being good

We continue to obsess over the issue of "goodness" in the context of leisure music pursuits such as collegiate a cappella. Our postscript interviewees' thoughts and opinions, while displaying the advantages of hindsight, did not necessarily provide the simple clarity we hoped we might find. It is probably a fool's errand to believe that a perfect mix of "musical" and "social" practice is possible. The

---

[3] Private club membership has always been about establishing status and separating members from larger communities. Despite a myriad of US federal laws that explicitly prohibit discrimination on the basis of race, it has remained "legal" to exclude. A recent article in *Sports Illustrated* (https://www.si.com/golf/2019/07/01/private-golf-clubs-muirfield-augusta-women-discrimination, accessed June 1, 2020) provides context as to how prominent golf courses and private clubs continue to legally deny entry to women, African Americans, Catholics, Jews, and other demographic classifications. The author explains that the Civil Rights Act of 1964 contains an exemption for private clubs in their membership activities. Citing that the Act "shall not apply to a private club or other establishment not in fact open to the public, except to the extent that the facilities of such establishment are made available to the customers or patrons of an establishment." This language means that though private clubs can't discriminate against customers, they can discriminate against prospective members. "Those choices have often arisen in the wake of sustained public pressure or having to confront the prospect of diminished revenue. Put differently, a decision to change a discriminatory membership policy doesn't automatically prove an actual change in attitude."

best one can hope for is to, as Derek so eloquently put it, "average the 'want' in the group," by which he meant grappling with the elusive balance of effort and desired musical standards.

Barry, one of the few music majors among our original informants, illuminated the dangers of failing to recognize perspective. "The [school of music] really drove me away from music," he admitted. Although Barry continues to use music in a leisure capacity and is still passionately involved in various ways, he recognized upon graduation with his master's degree that he would likely be very unhappy with music as his full-time vocation/occupation and therefore sought out a career outside of music. Barry's story is helpful in clarifying the difference between being "the best" and being "good enough." Schools (conservatories) of music in the United States (and likely most areas of the world) continue to operate on a principle of excellence whereby the only measure of success in music is demonstrated through occupation/employment, something that requires being the best (i.e., "winning" a job). This is understandable, of course. Bachelor of Music degrees are "professional" (rather than "liberal") in nature. One almost always enters such a degree program with an expectation of gainful employment related to the course of study (i.e., music), something that invariably demands placing the achievement of high musical standards above all else. Music, however, is not like chemical engineering or marketing. Music is special in this sense. One might hope that it is possible to study music formally in a way that does not sap it of its life-affirming, well-being potential.

Collegiate a cappella members do not "study" music in the way that music students do; they only "participate" in it. But of course they still need to rehearse (learn) the arrangements in order to present performances publicly. And therein lies the rub. As discussed in Chapter 2, the locus of enjoyment in collegiate a cappella differs between people. The "level of intensity" can be a turn-on or a turnoff, depending on how "being good" is approached. Despite how he felt about his school of music experience, Barry, for example, still believes "it is always important to be excellent." With a touch of irony, perhaps, he added that he has always operated according to the mantra "Be the best or don't try at all." What made this work for his a cappella group, he pointed out, was that they were "lucky to be talented enough" that they "didn't have to try too hard."

Other interviewees expressed that, in retrospect, they were too serious about trying to be good at the time. Derek suggested that "a cappella folks get so caught up in their world" that they lose perspective. In his own case, he confessed that he was guilty of this as an undergraduate. He described how he joined his group "with high commitment, practicing two to three hours a day." Upon becoming music director, he didn't think the group was as good as he wanted them to be and pushed them to be better. The members eventually revolted, telling him his efforts were "making it not fun anymore." Similarly, Craig told us that, looking back, he wished his group was more relaxed. For example, they "did ICCAs every year," something that added stress to the experience. His first two years in the group were especially intense, he said, due to the necessary choreography sessions (which he strongly disliked). He would have preferred "to just hang out" instead. Leslie's comments largely echoed Craig's:

> Looking back, we didn't need to be good. I was in it to sing and have a good time. You don't want to be embarrassed. When I look back, I don't think about how well we did it; I think about how fun it was to do it. [Performing well] was a level of stress we did not need to put on ourselves. We could have just had a good time. (Leslie)

None of this is to imply our interviewees now believed their a cappella experiences should have been casual or nonserious—something evident in Leslie's mention of not wanting to be embarrassed. Almost all interviewees made a point of emphasizing the importance of working toward something and having a purpose. Julie, for instance, spoke about "having a business-like attitude during rehearsals and then having fun afterwards." The role of the ICCAs continued to divide opinion, however. Some responses were critical of the judging criteria, which some thought were too subjective (mostly due to the choreography element), and the undue stress it placed on groups (e.g., "not sure if we could beat the Nor'easters anyways, so what was the point?"). Others felt positively about the experience, describing it in terms of an accomplishment. Michelle, for example, recalled the sense of relief the group felt when they finished third in a regional round one year. They were thrilled to have done so well but also relieved they didn't do well enough to move on to the next round because everyone was "so burnt out" by that point.

Wayne Booth writes that what drives amateuring is the "doing-for-the-love-of doing" (1999, 13), not hard work toward some abstract future goal. Unlike so much of school music learning, which epitomizes Booth's critique about abstract goals—that is, the idea that one learns music because it is good for you rather than good to do—the ICCAs, like school music competitions, represent a concrete goal. This likely helps to explain their appeal for some people. At the same time, we wonder if the "love-of-doing" for participants becomes distorted through ICCA participation, in that the "doing" becomes less about singing with friends and more about "doing competition." Being good, in other words, shifts from an intrinsic to an instrumental motivator. One needs to be good in order to win rather than to increase the feeling of enjoyment in the activity.

Musical agency

> Looking at sheet music now, I can still read it. I'm a little bit rusty and it takes a little bit longer and it's not quite as natural. So I think I would categorize myself as someone who can re-tap the skills when needed. (Nate)

> I think that's something I'm dealing with right now, music directing this law school group, is that nobody was a music major in undergrad. Only half of us read music and those of us that do read rather slowly. That makes the experience no less meaningful. (Jake)

In Chapter 6, we considered the extent to which school music programs develop sufficient "interdependent" musical agency in order for people to make music without the aid of a more knowledgeable other (i.e., a trained music leader). As we have discussed in this book, collegiate a cappella groups throughout the United States and Canada manage to arrange, rehearse, and perform music to a level sufficient to sustain the interest of their participants despite not having "professional" (i.e., formally trained) musical leadership. And while it may be true that the level of musical sophistication and performance level varies widely from group to group, even those at the less "musically advanced" end of the continuum still manage to make music in a way that warrants interest and enjoyment among members. Given our explication of agency (solo, proxy, interdependent), we were curious about our interviewees' thoughts on what they felt was important in terms of the musical knowledge and skills necessary to enable their ongoing musical interests. Predictably, perhaps, responses to this line of questioning varied widely. Several pointed out that, when it comes to a musical practice like a cappella, it is critical to have people with a range of abilities. Not everyone needs to have a level of music theory necessary to produce arrangements, but at least a couple of people do. Similarly, not everyone needs to know how to effectively lead a group through rehearsals, but at least one person does. Julie suggested that, when it comes to the basic ability to match the pitch and rhythm of the person next to you, or being able to carry a harmonized musical line, collegiate a cappella might hone the skill but a complete novice without such abilities isn't likely to learn it in collegiate a cappella—a point that speaks to the fact that (1) collegiate a cappella isn't a training ground, and (2) someone without such abilities isn't likely to pass the audition in the first place. Collegiate a cappella, in other words, presumes musical abilities that must be deliberately developed, or in rare cases "naturally occurring," prior to college.

Based on our study, we estimate only a small percentage of collegiate a cappella singers have no prior formal music study. The majority participated in some form of school music. It is not surprising, then, that so many participants appear to privilege fluency in music notation as a marker of being musically educated. As discussed in Chapter 2, most groups use notation for rehearsal purposes, much in the same way they likely did in secondary school, rather than viewing notation as but one of several possible mediating tools for learning arrangements. Only one group we observed opted for a purely rote-learning approach during rehearsals. In his postscript interview, Barry shared his recent experience of singing in groups without notation and being shocked at how fast groups can learn by rote compared with the analytic notation-centered approach he used to use with his collegiate a cappella group. Despite his master's degree in choral conducting, he proposed the idea—heretical to most people with formal musical training—that, compared with rote learning, "notation-dependency actually enfeebles people" who desire lifelong music making.

Staying Musically Active

> The reason I loved being in a cappella—doing it at that certain point of my life—is that it was unique to that specific time period. If I were to return to singing a cappella I would have to in my mind, understand that I would use the skills I developed during my college years, but that it wouldn't be the same. I wouldn't ever want to try to "relive the glory days" per se, because it simply won't be the same. This is not to say that it would have less meaning, but it certainly would be different. (Nate)

College activity or lifelong leisure activity? This was fundamentally what we wanted to find out when we began this inquiry in 2011. As we discussed in Chapter 7, answers to this question very much depend upon how participants conceptualize their own involvement. Many participants appear to share Nate's sentiments above: collegiate a cappella is something very tied to time and place. For others, however, life without music is like life without sunshine. We are at a bit of a loss to explain the frequency of ongoing musical activity reported by our postscript interviewees. Setting aside the two music teachers as outliers, six of nine people continue to be musically active on a regular basis, a proportion we consider higher than expected based on the number of our original informants who, at the time, predicted music participation would end upon graduation. The three who weren't regularly active still reported being casually active: two on guitar and one singing from time to time in a relative's choir. All three of the casually active interviewees can be safely described as music lovers to the extent they regularly attend music events, sing in the car, collect music-related memorabilia, and so on. As mentioned at the outset, our postscript interviews were drawn from a convenience sample, but one not targeted in any way with an expectation of ongoing music participation. (In Roger's case, he had had no contact with anyone since the original interviews many years prior and had no reason to believe the people contacted would be any more likely to be musically active than any other original informant.) Without diminishing the significance of such a high rate of ongoing musical participation, we regard this finding as somewhat of a fluke.

We also find it somewhat of a fluke that four of the postscript interviewees were or had been active in post-collegiate a cappella (one of the current music teachers we interviewed auditioned for a post-collegiate a cappella group but didn't get in)—especially considering the somewhat negative attitudes toward "post" expressed in so many of our original interviews. Leslie said that she had considered post-collegiate a cappella when she graduated, but that either it seemed too intense, which she didn't have time for, or groups didn't rehearse often enough and she was worried that the level of the group might not be musically satisfying. "I would be embarrassed to tell people I was in a group if it wasn't good enough," she confessed.

One of the most remarkable stories about staying musically active came from Julie, who, in our original interview in 2012, replied to our question about music beyond college graduation by saying, "It's terrible that it's ending, and I have no idea what I'm doing. I think singing ends, unfortunately." At the time, she was convinced that a cappella was a college activity that had its time and place. After graduating with her bachelor's degree, Julie went on to do a one-year master's degree and then landed a "good position" with a nonprofit company. After a year in the workforce, she was visiting her mother and expressing her lack of enthusiasm for life. As she recounted: "My mom looked at me and said, 'You need to sing!'" Julie explained how she then googled "Boston a cappella" that night and emailed several groups. One emailed back and invited her for an audition. She was accepted into the group. Two months later she was voted in as the music director and has never looked back.

Michelle was the first informant we introduced in this book. Recall that Michelle always loved singing as a child but, despite repeated auditions, was never accepted into her high school chorus even though she was a very good musician with high-level piano and trombone skills. The times with her collegiate a cappella group were "the best memories I have of college," she said. Despite a time-intensive occupation today, "music is still her outlet." With her guitar-playing boyfriend, she performs regularly as a duo in local coffee shops and freelance gigs, singing and playing piano. Roger asked her if she had ever considered doing post-collegiate a cappella. It turns out she had. Like five of the other postscript interviewees, she auditioned for a group shortly after graduating from college. She didn't get in.

The last interview we conducted for this book was with Mickey Rapkin (see Foreword). Given the many similarities we found between our study and what he wrote in *Pitch Perfect*, we wanted to see if there was anything more we could learn about collegiate a cappella and its significance for its participants. Rapkin reported to us that he isn't currently singing but that he would drop everything and reschedule his life for another weekend with his collegiate a cappella group, Cayuga's Waiters.

References

Adler, Adam. 2002. "A case of boys' experiences of singing in school." PhD dissertation, University of Toronto.

Alberti, Alexander. 2017. "Two-part harmony: Building relationships between contemporary a cappella groups and music faculty." College Music Society National Conference, San Antonio, TX, October 26–28.

Allsup, Randall Everett. 2016. *Remixing the classroom: Toward an open philosophy of music education*. Bloomington: Indiana University Press.

Anonymous. 2017. "Harvard proposal would ban fraternities and sororities." *Boston.com*, July 12, 2017. https://www.boston.com/news/local-news/2017/07/12/harvard-proposal-would-ban-fraternities-and-sororities, accessed June 1, 2020.

Arasi, Melissa. 2006. "Adult reflections on a high school choral music program: Perceptions of meaning and lifelong influence." PhD dissertation, Georgia State University.

Arnett, Jeffrey Jensen. 2002. *Readings on adolescence and emerging adulthood*. Upper Saddle River, NJ: Prentice Hall.

Averill, Gage. 2003. *Four parts, no waiting: A social history of American barbershop harmony, American musicspheres*. New York: Oxford University Press.

Baird, Brandon J., C. Kwang Sung, Elizabeth Erickson-DiRenzo, and Tara E. Mokhtari. 2018. "A preliminary study of vocal health among collegiate a cappella singers." *Journal of Voice*. doi: 10.1016/j.jvoice.2018.10.003.

Barad, Karen Michelle. 2007. *Meeting the universe halfway: Quantum physics and the entanglement of matter and meaning*. Durham: Duke University Press.

Bartolome, Sarah, and Melanie Stapleton. 2018. "'Can't I sing with the girls?': A transgender music educator's journey." In *Marginalized voices in music education*, edited by Brent Talbot, 114–36. New York: Routledge.

Bates, Vincent C. 2012. "Social class and school music." *Music Educators Journal* 98 (4):33–7.

Bates, Vincent C. 2017. "Critical social class theory for music education." *International Journal of Education & the Arts* 18 (7):1–24.

Belz, Mary Jane. 1994. "The German gesangverein as a model of life-long participation in music." PhD dissertation, University of Minnesota.

Berglin, Jacob. 2015. "'It's much more collaborative:' Democratic action in contemporary collegiate a cappella." *Bulletin of the Council for Research in Music Education* (205):51–69.

Berglin, Jacob. 2018. "Beyond the repertoire: Incorporating contemporary a cappella process into the secondary choir." *The Choral Journal* 58 (11):10–19.

Bond, Vanessa. 2018. "Like putting a circle with a square: A male alto's choral journey." In *Marginalized voices in music education*, edited by Brent Talbot, 137–52. New York: Routledge.

Booth, Wayne C. 1999. *For the love of it: Amateuring and its rivals*. Chicago: University of Chicago Press.

Bourdieu, Pierre. 1977. *Outline of a theory of practice*. Cambridge, MA: Cambridge University Press.

Bourdieu, Pierre. 1984. *Distinction: A social critique of the judgement of taste*. Cambridge, MA: Harvard University Press.

Bourdieu, Pierre. 1986. "The forms of capital." In *Handbook of theory and research for the sociology of education*, edited by John G. Richardson, 241–58. Westport, CT: Greenwood Press.

Bourdieu, Pierre. 1993. *Sociology in question*. London and Thousand Oaks, CA: Sage.

Bourdieu, Pierre, and Jean Claude Passeron. 1977. *Reproduction in education, society and culture*. London and Beverly Hills: Sage.

Bowen, Charles Kevin. 1995. "Adult community bands in the Southeastern United States: An investigation of current activity and background profiles of the participants." PhD, Florida State University.

Bowring, George Edward. 1952. "Utilization of high school musical experiences in adult life, a study of selected graduates of Beaverhead County High School." MME thesis, University of Montana.

Bradley, Deborah. 2007. "The sounds of silence: Talking race in music education." *Action, Criticism, and Theory for Music Education* 6 (4):132–62.

Brown, Heather, and Marjon van der Pol. 2015. "Intergenerational transfer of time and risk preferences." *Journal of Economic Psychology* 49:187–204.

Brown, Trent R. 2012. "Students' registration in collegiate choral ensembles: Factors that influence continued participation." *International Journal of Research in Choral Singing* 4 (1):80–6.

Bull, Anna. 2019. *Class, control, and classical music*. New York: Oxford University Press.

Burch, Stephen. 2016. "Beyond the bell: Young adult former instrumental music student non-participation in community band or orchestra." DMA dissertation, Boston University.

Burlin, Thomas B. 2015. "High school contemporary a cappella: A descriptive phenomenology." PhD dissertation, University of North Texas.

Busch, Maria. 2005. "Predictors of lifelong learning in music: A survey of individuals participating in ensembles at community colleges in Illinois." PhD dissertation, University of Illinois at Urbana-Champaign.

Butler, Judith. 1990. *Gender trouble: Feminism and the subversion of identity*. New York: Routledge.

Butler, Judith. 1993. *Bodies that matter: On the discursive limits of "sex."* New York: Routledge.

Butler, Judith. 1999. *Gender trouble: Feminism and the subversion of identity*. 10th anniversary ed. New York: Routledge.

Carlsson, Fredrik, Dinky Daruvala, and Olof Johansson-Stenman. 2005. "Are people inequality-averse, or just risk-averse?" *Economica* 72 (287):375–96.

Carp, Randi Sue. 2004. "Single gender choral ensembles, attitudes and practices: A survey of Southern California high school choir directors." DMA dissertation, University of Southern California.

Castelli, Perry Anthony. 1986. "Attitudes of vocal music educators and public secondary school students on selected factors which influence a decline in male enrollment occurring between elementary and secondary public school vocal music programs." PhD dissertation, University of Maryland.

Chang, Jeff. 2014. *Who we be: The colorization of America*. New York: St. Martin's Press.

Chiodo, Patricia. 1997. "The development of lifelong commitment: A qualitative study of adult instrumental music participation (adult learners)." PhD dissertation, State University of New York at Buffalo.

Clothier, Richard Iven. 1967. "Factors influencing freshmen with high school band experience to elect or not to elect band membership at five liberal arts colleges in Iowa." EdD dissertation, University of Northern Colorado.

Coffin, Janice. 2005. "Why did we join? Why have we stayed? Membership in a women's barbershop chorus: A narrative inquiry into leadership, learning, and the development of voice through singing." MEd master's thesis, University of Prince Edward Island.

Coffman, Don D. 1996. "Musical backgrounds and interests of active older adult band members." *Dialogue in Instrumental Music Education* 20 (1):25–34.

Coffman, Don D. 2002a. "Banding together: New Horizons in lifelong music making." *Journal of Aging & Identity* 7 (2):133–43.

Coffman, Don D. 2002b. "Music and quality of life in older adults." *Psychomusicology—A Journal of Research in Music Cognition* 18:76–88.

Coffman, Don D. 2008. "Survey of New Horizons International Music Association musicians." *International Journal of Community Music* 1 (3):375–90.

Conner, Lynne. 2008. "In and out of the dark: A theory about audience behavior from Sophocles to spoken word." In *Engaging art: The next great transformation of America's cultural life*, edited by Steven J. Tepper and Bill J. Ivey, 103–24. New York: Routledge.

Creech, Andrea, Susan Hallam, Hilary Mcqueen, and Maria Varvarigou. 2013. "The power of music in the lives of older adults." *Research Studies in Music Education* 35 (1):87–102.

Dabback, William. 2007. "Toward a model of adult music learning as a socially-embedded phenomenon." PhD dissertation, University of Rochester.

Demorest, Steven M. 2000. "Encouraging male participation in chorus." *Music Educators Journal* 86 (4):38–41.

DeNora, Tia. 2000. *Music in everyday life*. New York: Cambridge University Press.

Duchan, Joshua S. 2007. "Collegiate a cappella: Emulation and originality." *American Music* 25 (4):477–506.

Duchan, Joshua S. 2012a. *Powerful voices: The musical and social world of collegiate a cappella*. Ann Arbor, MI: University of Michigan Press.

Duchan, Joshua S. 2012b. "Recordings, technology, and discourse in collegiate a cappella." *Journal of American Folklore* 125 (3):488–502.

Elpus, Ken, and Carlos Rodriguez Abril. 2011. "High school music ensemble students in the United States: A demographic profile." *Journal of Research in Music Education* 59 (2):128–45. doi: 10.1177/0022429411405207.

Elpus, Kenneth. 2015. "Music teacher licensure candidates in the United States." *Journal of Research in Music Education* 63 (3):314–35. doi: 10.1177/0022429415602470.

Emirbayer, Mustafa, and Ann Mische. 1998. "What is agency?" *American Journal of Sociology* 103 (4):962–1023.

Engelmayer, Caroline, and Michael Xie. 2018. "As sanctions take effect, sorority interest halves." *The Harvard Crimson*, February 5, 2018. https://www.thecrimson.com/article/2018/2/5/sorority-interest-dips/?utm_source=thecrimson&utm_medium=web_primary&utm_campaign=recommend_sidebar, accessed June 1, 2020.

Faivre-Ransom, Judy Lynn. 2001. "An investigation of factors that influence adult participation in music ensembles based on various behavioral theories: A case study of the Norfolk Chorale." DMA Dissertation, Shenandoah Conservatory.

Falkner, Kenneth Warren. 1957. "The influence of music education and private study on adult interest in music in two selected communities." PhD dissertation, The University of Iowa.

Faulkner, Robert, and Jane W. Davidson. 2006. "Men in chorus: Collaboration and competition in homo-social vocal behaviour." *Psychology of Music* 34 (2):219–37. doi: 10.1177/0305735606061853.

Finnegan, Ruth H. 1989. *The hidden musicians: Music-making in an English town*. Cambridge and New York: Cambridge University Press.

Foucault, Michel. 1982. "The subject and power." *Critical Inquiry* 8 (4):777–95.

Freer, Patrick K. 2006. "Hearing the voices of adolescent boys in choral music: A self-story." *Research Studies in Music Education* 27 (1):69–81.

Freer, Patrick K. 2007. "Between research and practice: How choral music loses boys in the 'middle.'" *Music Educators Journal* 94 (2):28–34.

Freer, Patrick K. 2008. "Boys' changing voices in the first century of MENC journals." *Music Educators Journal* 95 (1):41–7. doi: 10.1177/0027432108321076.

Freer, Patrick K. 2009. "Boys' descriptions of their experiences in choral music." *Research Studies in Music Education* 31 (2):142–60.

Freer, Patrick K. 2010. "Two decades of research on possible selves and the 'missing males' problem in choral music." *Das Fehlen männlicher Stimmen in der Chorausbildung* 28 (1):17–30.

Garnett, Liz. 2005. *The British barbershopper: A study in socio-musical values*. Aldershot, Hants, England and Burlington, VT: Ashgate.

Gates, J. Terry. 1989. "A historical comparison of public singing by American men and women." *Journal of Research in Music Education* 37 (1):32–47.

Gaztambide-Fernández, Rubén. 2010. "Wherefore the musicians?" *Philosophy of Music Education Review* 18 (1):65–84.

Goodrich, Andrew. 2019. "Spending their leisure time: Adult amateur musicians in a community band. Music education research." *Music Education Research* 21 (2): 174–84. doi: 10.1080/14613808.2018.1563057.

Graham, Roderick. 2009. "The function of music education in the growth of cultural openness in the USA." *Music Education Research* 11 (3):283–302.

Green, Lucy. 2001. *How popular musicians learn: A way ahead for music education.* Burlington, VT: Ashgate.

Griffin, Drew Blake. 2017. "All I need is the air I breathe: Music, media, and the practice of collegiate a cappella." MM thesis, The Florida State University.

Griffith, Martha Jayne. 2006. "Personality traits and musical interests of adult learners in an instrumental music program." PhD dissertation, The University of Oklahoma.

Hall, Clare. 2018. *Masculinity, class and music education: Boys performing middle-class masculinities through music.* New York and Secaucus, NJ: Palgrave Macmillan.

Hallam, Susan. 2015. *The power of music.* London, UK: International Music Education Research Centre.

Hallam, Susan, Andrea Creech, and Maria Varvarigou. 2016. "Well-being and music leisure activities through the lifespan: A psychological perspective." In *The Oxford handbook of music making and leisure*, edited by Roger Mantie and Gareth Dylan Smith, 31–60. New York: Oxford University Press.

Hallam, Susan, Creech, Andrea, Varvarigou, Maria and McQueen, Hilary. 2012. "The characteristics of older people who engage in community music making, their reasons for participation and the barriers they face." *Journal of Adult and Continuing Education* 18 (2):21–43. doi: 10.7227/JACE.18.2.3.

Haning, Marshall. 2019. ""Everyone has a voice": Informal learning in student-led collegiate a cappella ensembles." *Bulletin of the Council for Research in Music Education* (219):61–76.

Harding, Thomas Spencer. 1971. *College literary societies: Their contribution to higher education in the United States, 1815–1876.* New York: Pageant Press International.

Harrison, Scott D. 2007. "A perennial problem in gendered participation in music: What's happening to the boys?" *British Journal of Music Education* 24 (3):367–80.

Harrison, Scott D. 2008. *Masculinities and music: Engaging men and boys in making music.* Newcastle upon Tyne: Cambridge Scholars.

Hawkins, Patrick J. 2007. "What boys and girls learn through song: A content analysis of gender traits and sex bias in two choral classroom textbooks." *Research & Issues in Music Education* 5.

Heintzelman, T.D. 1988. "Adult concert band participation in the United States." DME dissertation, Indiana University.

Hess, Juliet. 2015. "Upping the "anti-": The value of an anti-racist theoretical framework in music education." *Action, Criticism, and Theory for Music Education* 14 (1):66–92.

Hess, Juliet. 2017. "Equity and music education: Euphemisms, terminal naivety, and whiteness." *Action, Criticism, and Theory for Music Education* 16 (3):15–47.

Hewson, Martin. 2010. "Agency." In *Encyclopedia of case study research*, edited by Albert J. Mills, Gabrielle Durepos and Elden Wiebe, 13–16. Thousand Oaks, CA: Sage.

Hoffman, Adria. 2013. "Compelling questions about music, education, and socioeconomic status." *Music Educators Journal* 100 (1):63–8.

Holmquist, Solveig. 1995. "A study of community choir members' school experiences." DMA dissertation, University of Oregon.

Holz, Emil. 1962. "The schools band contest of America." *Journal of Research in Music Education* 10 (1):3–12.

Hryshko, Dmytro, María José Luengo-Prado, and Bent E. Sørensen. 2011. "Childhood determinants of risk aversion: The long shadow of compulsory education." *Quantitative Economics* 2:37–72.

Ingraham, Chrys. 1994. "The heterosexual imaginary: Feminist sociology and theories of gender." *Sociological Theory* 12 (2):203–19. doi: 10.2307/201865.

Jackson, Jenna Leigh. 2009. "High school students' attitudes toward single-sex choir versus mixed choir." MM thesis, Louisiana State University and Agricultural and Mechanical College.

Jackson, Stevi. 2006. "Gender, sexuality and heterosexuality." *Feminist Theory* 7 (1):105–21.

Jellison, Judith A. 2000. "How can all people continue to be involved in meaningful music participation?" In *Vision 2020: The Housewright Symposium on the Future of Music Education*, 111–36. Reston, VA: MENC-The National Association for Music Education.

Jones, Jeremy D. 2010. "The development of collegiate male glee clubs in America: An historical overview." DMA dissertation, University of Cincinnati.

Jones, P.M. 2009. "Lifewide as well as lifelong: Broadening primary and secondary school music education's service to students' musical needs." *International Journal of Community Music* 2 (2&3):201–14.

Jorgensen, Nancy, and Catherine Pfeiler. 2008. "Successful single-sex offerings in the choral department." *Music Educators Journal* 94 (5):36–40. doi: 10.1177/00274321080940050109.

Kaplan, Max. 1993. *Barbershopping: Musical and social harmony.* London and Rutherford, NJ: Fairleigh Dickinson University Press and Associated University Presses.

Karlsen, Sidsel. 2011. "Using musical agency as a lens: Researching music education from the angle of experience." *Research Studies in Music Education* 33 (2):107–21.

Keating, Bevan. 2004. "A choral organizational structure for the developing male singer." DMA dissertation, The Ohio State University.

Keene, James A. 1982. *A history of music education in the United States.* Hanover, NH: University Press of New England.

Kennedy, Mary. 2002. "It's cool because we like to sing: Junior high school boys' experience of choral music as an elective." *Research Studies in Music Education* 18:26–37.

Kingsbury, Henry. 1988. *Music, talent, and performance: A conservatory cultural system.* Philadelphia: Temple University Press.

Kivy, Peter. 1991. "Music and the liberal education." *Journal of Aesthetic Education* 25 (3):79–93.

Kokotsaki, Dimitra, and Susan Hallam. 2011. "The perceived benefits of participative music making for non-music university students: A comparison with music students." *Music Education Research* 13 (2):149–72. doi: 10.1080/14613808.2011.577768.

Koza, Julia. 1992. "Picture this: Sex equity in textbook illustrations." *Music Educators Journal* 78 (7):28–33.

Koza, Julia. 1993. "The 'missing males' and other gender issues in music education: Evidence from the Music Supervisors Journal." *Journal of Research in Music Education* 41 (3):212–32.

Koza, Julia. 2008. "Listening for whiteness: Hearing cultural politics in undergraduate school music." *Philosophy of Music Education Review* 16 (2):145–55.

Kratus, John. 2007. "Music education at the tipping point." *Music Educators Journal* 94 (2):42–8. doi: 10.1177/002743210709400209.

Lamb, Roberta. 1996. "Discords: Feminist pedagogy in music education." *Theory into Practice* 35 (2):124–131.

Larson, Paul Sharpe 1983. "An exploratory study of lifelong musical interest and activity: Case studies of twelve retired adults." DMA dissertation, Temple University.

Lave, Jean, and Etienne Wenger. 1991. *Situated learning: Legitimate peripheral participation*. New York: Cambridge University Press.

Lawrence, Sidney, and Nadia Dachinger. 1967. "Factors relating to carryover of music training into adult life." *Journal of Research in Music Education* 15 (1):23–31.

Lloyd, Moya. 2005. *Beyond identity politics: Feminism, power and politics*. Thousand Oaks, CA: Sage.

Lonnberg, Evelynne Dreger. 1960. "The influence of secondary music education on adult musical participation." MA thesis, The Ohio State University.

Lucas, Mark. 2007. "Adolescent males' motivations to enroll or not enroll in choir." PhD dissertation, University of Oklahoma.

Maidlow, Sarah, and Rosemary Bruce. 1999. "The role of psychology research in understanding the sex/gender paradox in music—plus ça change." *Psychology of Music* 27 (2):147–58.

Mantie, Roger. 2012a. "Learners or participants? The pros and cons of lifelong learning." *International Journal of Community Music* 5 (3):217–35.

Mantie, Roger. 2012b. "A study of community band participants: Implications for music education." *Bulletin of the Council for Research in Music Education* (191):21–43.

Mantie, Roger. 2013. "Structure and agency in university-level recreational music making." *Music Education Research* 15 (1):39–58. doi: 10.1080/14613808.2012.722076.

Mantie, Roger, and Brent Talbot. 2015. "How can we change our habits if we don't talk about them?" *Action, Criticism, and Theory for Music Education* 14 (1):128–53.

Mantie, Roger, and Leonard Tan. 2019. "A cross-cultural examination of lifelong participation in community wind bands through the lens of organizational theory." *Journal of Research in Music Education* 67 (1):106–26. doi: 10.1177/0022429418820340.

Mantie, Roger, and Lynn Tucker. 2008. "Closing the gap: Does music-making have to stop upon graduation?" *International Journal of Community Music* 1 (2):217–27.

McClary, Susan. 1991. *Feminine endings: Music, gender, and sexuality*. Minneapolis: University of Minnesota Press.

Millar, Brett. 2008. "Selective hearing: Gender bias in the music preferences of young adults." *Psychology of music* 36 (4):429–45.

Mizener, Charlotte, P. 1993. "Attitudes of children toward singing and choir participation and assessed singing skill." *Journal of Research in Music Education* 41 (3):233–45.

Moder, Jennifer Ann. 2013. "Factors influencing non-music majors' decisions to participate in collegiate bands." PhD dissertation, University of Missouri—Kansas City.

Moore, Derek G., Karen Burland, and Jane W. Davidson. 2003. "The social context of musical success: A developmental account." *British Journal of Psychology* 94 (4):529–49. doi: 10.1348/000712603322503088.

Mountford, Richard Dean. 1977. "Significant predictors of college band participation by college freshmen with high school band experience." PhD dissertation, The Ohio State University.

Myers, David. 1995. "Lifelong learning: An emerging research agenda for music education." *Research Studies in Music Education* 4:21–7.

Myers, David. 2008a. "Freeing music education from schooling: Toward a lifespan perspective on music learning and teaching." *International Journal of Community Music* 1 (1):49–61.

Myers, David. 2008b. "Lifespan engagement and the question of relevance: Challenges for music education research in the twenty-first century." *Music Education Research* 10 (1):1–14. doi: 10.1080/14613800701871330.

Nazareth, T. C. 1998. "Achieving lifelong music education: Cooperation, coordination, and coherence." *General Music Today* 11 (2):21–3.

Neal, Charles. 1949. "Carry-over of musical activities following graduation from high school." PhD dissertation, Indiana University.

Neil, Ronald J. 1944. "The development of the competition-festival in music education." PhD dissertation, George Peabody College for Teachers.

Nettl, Bruno. 1995. *Heartland excursions: Ethnomusicological reflections on schools of music*. Urbana: University of Illinois Press.

O'Leary, Jared, and Evan Tobias. 2016. "Sonic participatory cultures within, through, and around video games." In *The Oxford handbook of music making and leisure*, edited by Roger Mantie and Gareth Dylan Smith, 541–64. New York: Oxford University Press.

O'Toole, Patricia. 1998. "A missing chapter from choral methods books: How choirs neglect girls." *The Choral Journal* 39 (5):9–32.

O'Toole, Patricia. 2000. "Music matters: Why I don't feel included in these musics or matters." *Bulletin of the Council for Research in Music Education* (144):28–39.

Ordway, Claire. 1964. "Music activities of high school graduates in two communities." *Journal of Research in Music Education* 12 (2):172–76.

Ortner, Sherry B. 2006. *Anthropology and social theory: Culture, power, and the acting subject.* Durham: Duke University Press.

Palkki, Joshua. 2015. "Gender trouble: Males, adolescence, and masculinity in the choral context." *The Choral Journal* 56 (4):24–35.

Palkki, Joshua. 2017. "Inclusivity in action: Transgender students in the choral classroom." *Choral Journal* 57 (11):20–34.

Palkki, Joshua, and Paul Caldwell. 2018. "'We are often invisible': A survey on safe space for LGBTQ students in secondary school choral programs." *Research Studies in Music Education* 40 (1):28–49.

Paparo, Stephen A. 2013. "The Accafellows: Exploring the music making and culture of a collegiate a cappella ensemble." *Music Education Research* 15 (1):19–38.

Parker, Elizabeth. 2009. "Understanding the process of social identity development in adolescent high school choral singers: A grounded theory." PhD dissertation, University of Nebraska-Lincoln.

Pate, Joseph A., and Corey W. Johnson. 2013. "Sympathetic chords: Reverberating connection through the lived leisure experiences of music listening." *International Journal of Community Music* 6 (2):189–203.

Patel, Leigh. 2016. *Decolonizing educational research: From ownership to answerability.* New York: Routledge.

Patterson, Frank Chester. 1985. "Motivational factors contributing to participation in community bands of the Montachusett region of North Central Massachusetts." PhD dissertation, University of Connecticut.

Patton, Marcia. 2008. "Choral music in the junior high/middle school: An argument for separating boy and girl choirs." *The Choral Journal* 49 (5):67–8.

Pitts, Stephanie. 2005. *Valuing musical participation.* Aldershot, Hants, England and Burlington, VT: Ashgate.

Pitts, Stephanie. 2009. "Roots and routes in adult musical participation: Investigating the impact of home and school on lifelong musical interest and involvement." *British Journal of Music Education* 26 (3):241–56. doi: 10.1017/S0265051709990088.

Pitts, Stephanie. 2012a. *Chances and choices: Exploring the impact of music education.* New York: Oxford University Press.

Pitts, Stephanie. 2012b. *Chances and choices: Exploring the impact of music education.* New York: Oxford University Press.

Pitts, Stephanie. 2016. "'The violin in the attic': Investigating the long-term value of lapsed musical participation." In *The Oxford handbook of music making and leisure*, edited by Roger Mantie and Gareth Dylan Smith, 171–86. New York: Oxford University Press.

Pitts, Stephanie. 2017. "What is music education for? Understanding and fostering routes into lifelong musical engagement." *Music Education Research* 19 (2):160–8. doi: 10.1080/14613808.2016.1166196.

Pitts, Stephanie, and Katharine Robinson. 2016. "Dropping in and dropping out: Experiences of sustaining and ceasing amateur participation in classical music." *British Journal of Music Education* 33 (3):327–46.

Pitts, Stephanie, Katharine Robinson, and Kunshan Goh. 2015. "Not playing any more: A qualitative investigation of why amateur musicians cease or continue membership of performing ensembles." *International Journal of Community Music* 8 (2):129–47. doi: 10.1386/ijcm.8.2.129_1.

Power, Anne. 2008. "What motivates and engages boys in music education?" *Bulletin of the Council for Research in Music Education* (175):85–102.

Rapkin, Mickey. 2008. *Pitch perfect: The quest for collegiate a cappella glory*. New York: Gotham Books.

Rapkin, Mickey. 2017. "The great Ivy League a cappella hazing scandal." *GQ*, November 2, 2017. https://www.gq.com/story/cornell-a-cappella-hazing-scandal, accessed June 1, 2020.

Reed, Jonathan. 2004. "Just start one: Strategies for implementing a male chorus in your choral program." *Choral Journal* 44 (7):63–5.

Regelski, Thomas. 2005. "Music and music education: Theory and praxis for 'making a difference.'" *Educational Philosophy and Theory* 37 (1):7–27.

Regelski, Thomas. 2006. "Reconnecting music education with society." *Action, Criticism, and Theory for Music Education* 5 (2).

Regelski, Thomas. 2007. "Amateuring in music and its rivals." *Action, Criticism, and Theory for Music Education* 6 (3):22–50.

Regelski, Thomas. 2009. "Curriculum reform: Reclaiming 'music' as social praxis." *Action, Criticism, and Theory for Music Education* 8 (1): 66–84.

Regelski, Thomas. 2012. "Musicianism and the ethics of school music." *Action, Criticism, and Theory for Music Education* 11 (1):7–42.

Rich, Adrienne. 1980. "Compulsory heterosexuality and lesbian existence." *Signs* 5 (4):631–60.

Roe, Paul F. 1970. *Choral music education*. Englewood Cliffs, NJ, Prentice-Hall.

Rohrer, Thomas P. 2002. "The debate on competition in music in the twentieth century." *Update: Applications of Research in Music Education* 21 (1):38–47.

Rohwer, Debbie. 2010. "Understanding adult interests and needs: The pitfalls in wanting to know." *International Journal of Community Music* 3 (2):203–12. doi: 10.1386/ijcm.3.2.203_1.

Rohwer, Debbie, and Don D. Coffman. 2007. "Relationships between wind band membership, activity level, spirituality and quality of life in older adults." *Research Perspectives in Music Education* 10:21–7.

Schatzki, Theodore R. 1996. *Social practices: A Wittgensteinian approach to human activity and the social*. Cambridge and New York: Cambridge University Press.

Schatzki, Theodore R. 2002. *The site of the social: A philosophical account of the constitution of social life and change*. University Park, PA: Pennsylvania State University Press.

Seago, Ted. 1993. "Motivational factors influencing participation in selected Southern Baptist church choirs." EdD Dissertation, University of Houston.

Sharon, Deke. 2018. *So you want to sing a cappella: A guide for performers*. Lanham, MD: Rowman & Littlefield.

Slutsky, Corey Brian. 2005. "Music without instruments: The growth and explosion of a cappella music over the last 10 to 15 years." MA thesis, University of Southern California.

Small, Christopher. 1998. *Musicking: The meanings of performing and listening*. Hanover: University Press of New England.

Spell, Gwynelle. 1989. "Motivational factors and selected socio-demographic characteristics of Georgia community chorus participants as measured by the education participation scale, the community chorus participation scale, and the personal inventory form." EdD dissertation, University of Georgia.

Spencer, William. 1996. "An attitude assessment of amateur musicians in community bands." PhD Dissertation, University of North Texas.

St. Jean, Donald. 2014. "Perspectives on a cappella: A mixed methods portrait of the perceived benefits of unaccompanied ensemble singing on the development of the musical skills of undergraduate students." DMA dissertation, Boston University.

Stebbins, Robert A. 1996. *The barbershop singer: Inside the social world of a musical hobby*. Toronto and Buffalo: University of Toronto Press.

Stein, Gertrude Emilie. 1970. "A study of the relation of music instruction during secondary school years to adult musical status, as reflected in the activities interests and attitudes of recent high school graduates." PhD dissertation, University of Michigan.

Stewart, Jonathan David. 2016. "Six: Fluid leadership and aural arranging within the context of contemporary a cappella." DMA dissertation, Boston University.

Sweet, Bridget. 2010. "A case study: Middle school boys' perceptions of singing and participation in choir." *UPDATE: Applications of Research in Music Education* 28 (2):5–12.

Talbot, Brent. 2014. "A proleptic perspective of music education." In *Music education: Navigating the future*, edited by Clint Randles, 29–42. New York: Routledge.

Talbot, Brent. 2018a. "Introduction." In *Marginalized voices in music education*, edited by Brent Talbot, 1–12. New York: Routledge.

Talbot, Brent. 2018b. "Superdiversity in music education." In *Music education research in the 21st century: Theories, questions, problems, and methodological pluralism*, edited by Jay Dorfman and Diana Dansereau, 181–92. New York: Springer.

Talbot, Brent, and Roger Mantie. 2015. "Blinded by bureaucracy: The pitfalls of professionalization." In *Envisioning music teacher education*, edited by S. Conkling, 155–80. Lanham, MD: Rowman & Littlefield.

Tatum, Marielon Elaine. 1985. "A descriptive analysis of the status of music programs in selected retirement residences and senior citizens' centers in the Southeastern United States." DME dissertation, Indiana University.

Thaller, Gregg Philip. 1999. "The community contributions, recruitment, and retention practices of select adult community bands in Eastern Massachusetts." DME dissertation, University of Cincinnati.

Thornton, Darrin. 2010. "Adult music engagement: Perspectives from three musically engaged cases." PhD dissertation, Pennsylvania State University.

Tipps, James. 1992. "Profile characteristics and musical backgrounds of community chorus participants in the Southeast United States." PhD Dissertation, The Florida State University.

Tsugawa, Samuel. 2009. "Senior adult music learning, motivation, and meaning construction in two New Horizons ensembles." DMA dissertation, Arizona State University.

Turk, Diana B. 2004. *Bound by a mighty vow: Sisterhood and women's fraternities, 1870-1920*. New York: New York University Press.

Turton, Angela, and Colin Durrant. 2002. "A study of adults' attitudes, perceptions and reflections on their singing experience in secondary school: Some implications for music education." *British Journal of Music Education* 19 (1):31–48.

Valian, Virginia. 1998. *Why so slow?: The advancement of women*. Cambridge, MA: The MIT Press.

Van Ingen, Erik, and Koen Van Eijck. 2009. "Leisure and social capital: An analysis of types of company and activities." *Leisure Sciences* 31:192–206. doi: 10.1080/01490400802686078.

Vanderark, Sherman, Newman, Isadore, and Bell, Sarah 1983. "The effects of music participation on quality of life of the elderly." *Music Therapy Perspectives* 3:71–81.

Viggiano, F. Anthony. 1941. "Reaching the adolescent who thinks it's sissy to sing." *Music Educators Journal* 27 (5):62–3.

Waggoner, Robert 1971. "Factors relating to participation and non-participation in community performance groups at the level in Atlanta, Georgia." PhD dissertation, Florida State University.

Warner, Michael. 1991. "Introduction: Fear of a queer planet." *Social Text* (29):3–17.

Wenger, Etienne. 1998. *Communities of practice: Learning, meaning, and identity*. Cambridge, England: Cambridge University Press.

Williams, David A. 1996. "Competition and music—who are the winners? A review of the literature." *Update: Applications of Research in Music Education* 15 (1):16–21.

Williams, David A. 2007. "What are music educators doing and how well are we doing it?" *Music Educators Journal* 94 (1):18.

Williams, David A. 2011. "The elephant in the room." *Music Educators Journal* 98 (1):51–7. doi: 10.1177/0027432111415538.

Williams, Jana. 2011. "Male participation and male recruitment issues in middle and high school chorus." DMA dissertation, Boston University.

Winstead, J. Lloyd. 2013. *When colleges sang: The story of singing in American college life*. Tuscaloosa: University of Alabama Press.

Wise, George, David Hartmann, and J.F. Bradley. 1992. "Exploration of the relationship between choral singing and successful aging." *Psychological Reports* 70 (3c):1175–83.

Wittig, Monique. 1989. "On the social contract." *Feminist Issues* 9:3–12. doi: 10.1007/BF02685600.

Woody, Robert H., and Elizabeth C. Parker. 2012. "Encouraging participatory musicianship among university students." *Research Studies in Music Education* 34 (2):189–205. doi: 10.1177/1321103X12464857.

Wright, Ruth. 2008. "Kicking the habitus: Power, culture and pedagogy in the secondary school music curriculum." *Music Education Research* 10 (3):389–402.

Wright, Ruth. 2010. "Democracy, social exclusion and music education: Possibilities for change." In *Sociology and music education*, edited by Ruth Wright, 263–81. Burlington, VT: Ashgate.

Zemek, Michael D. 2010. "Where's the evidence? Finding support for separating middle and junior high school choirs by gender." *UPDATE: Applications of Research in Music Education* 29 (1):15–21.

Index

A Cappella League 111
abilities 2, 23, 30, 32, 42, 83, 101, 105, 106, 115, 120, 138
abuse 33, 72
access 80, 87, 88, 132. *See also* equity and inclusion 134
accessibility
    and equity 90
achievement 80, 136
admissions 66, 73, 81, 125–6
adulthood 6, 102, 114, 142
advantage 53, 73
    class 121
    male (sexual) 50, 57, 63–4
    systems of 65
    whiteness 134
aesthetic 109
    amateur 2, 10
    experience 92
    values 20
African American 132
agency 61, 64–5, 76, 91
    interdependent 103–5, 108, 110
    musical 6, 14, 93, 99–103, 120, 135, 138
    proxy 103–5
    solo 103–4
alumni 11, 123
    collegiate a cappella 9, 96, 127, 134
    Greek life 67
    reunions 118
amateurism 92–3, 97, 99, 107–8
arrangement 30, 41, 57
arranger 30, 94, 106
asymmetries 72
    gender 48
attitudes 72
    of higher education 96
    and perceptions of males 56
attraction 50, 56, 58
    same-sex 63
auditions 40, 63, 82, 84, 124, 140
authority 33, 35, 103

figure 102
    institutional 11
    musical expertise and 18, 29
autonomy 100. *See also* agency
avocational
    music making 9, 37, 99

barbershop 1, 10–12, 19, 74, 86, 111, 115–16
barrier 21, 93, 95, 127, 133
beatboxing 12, 42, 77
becoming
    a music teacher 89
Beelzebubs 11–12, 62
being good 18, 26–7, 33, 35, 37, 103, 120, 135–7
belonging. *See* bonding
benefit
    ancillary 25, 126
    cost- 27, 120
    financial 52
    leisure 92
    social 44
bias
    unconscious 132, 134
binaries
    cisgender 71
    gender 55
black barbershop 19
bonding 22, 25, 44, 70
Boston 13, 81, 123, 128, 133, 140
Bourdieu 5, 15, 75–81, 85, 87, 89
breakup 46–7
Butler 59–61, 64–5, 65

camaraderie 43, 45
capacities 78, 105, 110
capital 75–7, 81, 83–90
    cultural 73, 80, 86–90, 108, 126, 132, 133
    economic 80–1, 87, 90
    social 80, 153
    symbolic 80

Cayuga's Waiters 72, 141
championship 8, 13, 19. *See also* ICCAs
childhood 119, 147
choice 25, 42, 51, 61, 78, 81, 89, 119
choir 3–4, 11, 31, 49, 50, 56, 82, 103, 109, 116–17, 129, 139
　director 11, 31
choreo(graphy) 20, 48, 137
church choirs 111
cisgender 71. *See also* gender
class. *See also* diversity
　middle-upper 81, 84, 109, 121, 132–3
　and race 55, 66, 131
　social 80
classical 41, 81, 88, 90, 92, 110
co-ed group 12, 22, 30, 37, 40, 42, 45, 47, 52, 61–2, 64, 106, 130
college
　activity 114, 117, 139, 140
　experience 4, 65, 79, 86, 107, 114, 116, 120
　singing 132
commitment 22, 25–6, 81, 112–13, 117–18, 136
community
　band-orchestra listserve 92
　choir 103, 117
　music education 112
　service 116
compete 20, 22, 119. *See also* ICCAs
competence 29–31, 88, 101–3
competency 89, 102
competition 17–22, 34, 37, 42, 47, 50, 81, 83, 86, 124, 131, 135, 137
conducting 34, 56, 112, 139
conductor 2, 34, 104–5
confidence 50, 77, 107, 125
conservatories 86, 136. *See also* schools of music
conservatory model 89
continuity 7–9, 60
control 23, 101, 118
costuming 55, 121. *See also* gender
cover(s) 12, 115
criteria 20, 82, 84, 99, 137. *See also* judging
culture 33, 56, 58–9, 63, 70, 72, 74–5, 80, 88, 109–10, 124
curricular

co- 7, 10, 19, 51
extra 78–9, 87
curriculum 66, 92, 94,

de Beauvoir, Simone 58, 60. *See also* gender
democratic(ally) 33–4, 90
demographic(ally) 8, 87, 119, 135, 145
desire. *See also* motivation
　heterosexual 45, 56
　same-sex 62, 71
　sexual 47, 59
discrimination 14, 135
dispositions 6, 78, 93, 105, 110
distinction. *See* Bourdieu
diversity 82, 84–5, 131–5
drama 45, 63
drive. *See* motivation
Duchan 10, 12, 13, 75, 114

education
　choral 56
　higher 2, 66, 88–9
　of women 66
efficacy. *See* agency
effort. *See* being good
elementary school 9, 106, 129
embodiment. *See* habitus
emerging. *See* adulthood
employment 22, 92, 136
engagement
　musical 103
　lifelong 14, 89, 110
　lifespan 113
enjoyment
　locus of 17–18, 26, 28–9, 35–7, 120, 136
　musical 35
　recreational 35
　social 33
ensembles
　choral 4, 69, 95
　large 7, 93, 100
　recreational 104
　school 29, 101
　self-run 91
　single-sex 70
environment
　all-male 70
　co-ed 57, 71
　single-sex 44–5, 47

equality. *See also* inequality
   gender 49, 131
   social 84
equity
   and access 88
evaluation criteria 82
excellence 18, 27–8, 32–3, 35, 97, 120, 135–6
exchange. *See* Bourdieu, Capital
extracurricular 7, 78–9, 87
extrinsic 22–3

facilities 91, 97, 108, 135
faculty 10, 72, 94–6, 108, 123
failure. *See* locus of enjoyment
falsetto 48, 57
female
   all- 12, 14, 21–2, 30, 35, 39–52, 55, 57, 62, 64, 66–7, 70–1, 116, 128–31
femininity 47, 56, 68, 70, 130–1
field. *See* Bourdieu
foucault 60–1, 63, 65, 76, 78
fraternity 14, 66–7, 70–1, 114, 118, 129–31
friendship(s) 47, 129
fulfillment. *See* being good
fun. *See* being good; Motivation and desire

game. *See* field
gatekeeping 82, 84
gender
   asymmetries 48
   binaries 55
   hierarchies 39, 53
   inequality 60, 67, 121, 128, 131
   norms 58
   performativity 61
   and sexuality 39–55, 58–9, 61, 67–8, 72, 127–8, 130–1
   subjugation 51
girl(s) 39–44, 47, 49, 51, 61, 63, 64, 68–70. *See also* all-female
glee
   clubs 2, 19
   TV show 2, 11, 48, 94, 97, 124
goal. *See also* competence; motivation
   learning 99, 107, 137
   musical 18
   performance 29–31

good
   being 18, 26–7, 33, 35, 37, 103, 120, 135–7
   desire to be 27, 93
   enough 26–8, 35, 117, 120, 130, 136, 140
Googapella 74, 86
graduation 7, 107, 111–12, 115, 123, 123–49
guilty pleasure 24
guys 4, 26, 28–9, 40–5, 47, 49, 51, 61–4, 96, 106, 129–31. *See also* gender asymmetries
groups 41

habitus 75–9, 81, 84
hang out 4, 25, 44–5, 64, 70, 137
happiness 17, 28, 32–3, 35, 120
HBCUs 132
healthy
   activity 24
   singing 95–6
hegemony 99, 129
heteronormativity 55, 57–9, 63–4, 121
heterosexual 45, 47, 56, 58–9, 61–3
homosexuality. *See* heteronormativity
hierarchies 39–42, 53, 57, 71, 76, 130
hierarchy 40, 94, 121
Higher Education. *See* education
Hispanic 8, 132
hypermasculine 130
hypermasculinity 129–31

ICCA(s) 20–23, 27, 34, 79, 120, 133, 137
identity
   group 11, 20, 56, 70, 129–30
   sexual 56, 59, 68, 130
imagined futures 114–15, 117, 120
inclusion 87, 132, 134–5. *See also* access and inclusion
independence
   musical 30, 100–1, 104
   part 83, 105
independent
   learning 6, 14, 103
   music making 6, 14, 91, 101, 103

inequality
    gender 51, 55, 57, 59–61, 67, 71, 121, 128–31
    sexual 55, 59, 67, 71, 128
institutional
    authority 11
    choir 11, 116
    structures 13, 93
institutionalization 10, 88
institutionalized music 9, 27, 70, 93, 95, 110, 112, 116
intentionality 29, 108, 120
intercollegiate 19
interdependent 103–5, 108, 110. *See also* agency
interpersonal 37, 46, 125
intrinsic 22–3, 34. *See also* motivation
Ivy League 8, 11–12, 57, 71–4, 84, 92, 121, 125, 132, 151

leadership 30, 32, 72, 83, 126
    ensemble 30, 32–3
    musical 30, 103, 138
    strong 34
learning. *See* music learning
legitimization. *See* Bourdieu
lifelong
    involvement 6, 91, 101–2, 112
    music making 5, 8, 14–5, 45, 88, 91–5, 101, 103, 113, 118–9, 139
    participation 6, 9, 89, 92, 109–10, 113, 124
lifespan 113
lifestyle 7, 15, 78, 117, 121
liminal 7, 114, 119
loathing 94, 96, 108
locus of enjoyment 18, 26, 28–9, 35–7, 120, 136
Logarhythms 11, 75

male
    all- 4, 11–12, 22, 39–52, 55–8, 61–2, 64, 66, 67, 70–2, 115, 123–4, 128–31
    privilege 39, 41, 48, 50–2, 55, 57, 63, 65, 67, 121, 132
    sexual advantage 50, 53, 57, 63–4
masculine 56, 59, 70, 130
masculinist 129
masculinity 56, 61–2, 70, 129–31, 146, 150
MD. *See* music director

meritocracy. *See* capital
motivation. *See also* being good
    and desire 18, 22
    and enjoyment 29
    and excellence 18
    extrinsic 22–3
music
    classical 41, 81, 88, 90, 92, 110, 143, 151
    community 92, 109, 112, 117
    director 29–30, 32–3, 40, 44, 47, 104, 106, 116, 128, 136, 140
    learning 14–15, 89, 93, 95, 99, 107, 109, 112–13, 124, 137
    lifelong 5–6, 8, 14–15, 45, 88, 91–5, 98, 101–3, 110, 112–13, 118–19, 124, 139
    notation 31, 37, 49, 83, 101, 129, 139
    offerings 11, 93
    professors 45, 86, 88, 95
    programs 6, 8–9, 17, 23, 29–30, 82, 90, 93–4, 100–4, 109, 120–2, 134, 138, 144, 150, 152
    teachers 5–6, 8, 32–3, 68, 86, 88, 90, 94–6, 99–100, 106, 109, 121–2, 125, 139–40
    teacher associations 94, 121
    theory 10, 14, 23, 30, 80, 85, 90, 106–7, 113, 138
musical impact 5–6, 9, 93
musically active 1–3, 5, 93, 108, 123, 139
musicianism. *See* Regelski
musicians
    classical 88, 92
    collegiate 6, 13, 19, 29–30, 88, 94–5, 100, 105, 108, 113
    formally trained 95
    hidden 93
    professional 92, 101, 105, 108
    in the UK 6, 88, 93
musicianship 6, 29–30, 93–5, 101, 104, 108, 113
musicking 9, 99

NAfME 88
normalized. *See* gender
nostalgia 118, 125, 131
notation 31, 37, 83, 101, 139

omnivorousness 87, 89
organization(s) 2, 9, 12–13, 18–19, 65–7, 76–7, 92, 94, 111

partnership(s) 40, 46–7
patriarchy (patriarchal) 49, 51, 59, 121
Pentatonix 2, 57, 118, 126
perc. *See* beatboxing
performance
    excellence in 18
    goals 29–30
    levels 29
    practices 29, 50, 52
    standards 26
performativity 55, 58, 60–1, 71, 130
personality 11, 30, 84–5, 121
picking our friends 84
power
    brokers 88
    differentials 71
    and privilege 15
    relationships 64
    structures of 14–15, 109
presitige 73, 80
privilege
    of choice 81
    heterosexual 63
    male 41, 52, 55, 57, 67
    power and 15
    white 132
professional
    obligations 55, 68
    setting 36

quality
    performance 31, 35, 42, 55, 60–1, 71, 121, 134
    vocal 42, 55, 57
queer theory 59

race. *See* diversity
recorder 106
recording 13, 18, 31, 116
recreational
    activities 26, 34, 71
    enjoyment 35
    involvement 5, 23–4, 27, 85, 91, 98–9, 104
    leisure 24, 108, 119
    music makers 23, 28, 96
    music making 27, 88, 95, 98–9, 108, 110, 117
    musicians 19
    participation 118

pursuits 85
singing 2, 19, 96
Regelski 5–6, 93, 99–101, 108, 110, 112–13
rehearsal
    choices 31–2
    practices 32, 37, 122
    space 91, 97
    time 17, 27
rehearsing 1, 27–9, 31–2, 37, 63, 97
relations
    family 45, 47, 63, 80
    gender 45, 47, 58–9, 64, 67, 127–8, 130, 142
relationship(s)
    group 32
    power 64, 130
    sexual 45–7, 64
    social 80
repertoire
    choices 12, 95, 121
    quality 69, 88, 121
resist(ance) 11, 64, 68, 121
résumé(s) 34, 55, 86, 126, 138
reward 22
rhythm 30, 32, 83, 138
rhythmic 12, 32, 104–5
Rockapella 10, 12
rote learning 139

safe spaces 130
Schatzki 75–7
school
    high 3–4, 7–9, 15, 21, 30–2, 39, 51, 71, 81, 86, 94–5, 119, 129, 140
    music 1, 84, 91, 108, 123
    music experiences 8, 18, 29
    music teachers 5, 8, 32–3, 86, 88, 95, 122
schooling 8, 37, 68, 89, 92, 100, 102, 108, 124
secondary
    level 33, 93, 98
    school 5, 71, 139
selection process 81
sex
    -segregated 68–9, 71
    single 41, 44, 47
sexy 49, 51, 61–2
sheet music 31, 94, 138

shimmying 51
Silicon Valley 86, 88
sisterhood 45
skills
   interpersonal 125
   and knowledge 93, 101–2
   leadership 126
   musical 2, 101, 126
   performance 104
Snowcappella 86–7
sociability 24–5, 80, 83, 85
social
   dysfunction 135
   life 5, 63, 65, 82
   reproduction 37
societies 55, 65–6, 97, 111
solo(s) 3–4, 12, 18, 35, 102–3, 105, 110, 138
soloist 12, 21, 42, 106
sonority 41, 57
sorority (sororities) 44, 65–7, 70–2, 121
space(s)
   liminal 114
   rehearsal 91, 97
   safe 130
SPEBSQSA 10
standards
   academic 66
   double 52
   of excellence 97
   lower 69
   musical 20, 27, 35–7, 136
   performance 26
Stebbins 7, 19
stereotypes 47, 128
stigma 91, 98–9
stratification 123
   social 87
stress 3, 85, 137
structural
   conditions 78
   environments 102
   forces 53, 75–6, 134
structures
   of campus life 58
   curricular 2
   gendered 67
   of music education 15
   of participation 121
   of power 15, 109

success
   and enjoyment 29
   and failure 23
Sweet Adelines 111

tastes 5, 12, 19
   musical 12
tech
   sector 86
techapella 86
temporal. *See* musical agency
tour(s, ed, ing) 81–2, 86
trans(gender)
   singers 56
truth
   regimes of 61

unconscious. *See* bias
undergraduate
   enrollment 132
   experience 112
   music major 107
   singer 97
   years 125, 135
underrepresentation
   of males 69
unhealthy
   singing 95–6
univore 89

value. *See* capital
varsity. *See* sports
veterans 65
Victorian ideals 66
vocal
   health 41, 95
   practices 95
   preferences 42
   quality 57
   range 41, 83
voice
   faculty 95
   healthy 41, 95
   nature of 122
   teacher 95
volitional
   choices 119
   involvement 135
   music making 2, 5

wealthy families 66, 73
Western
    art music 69, 86, 87, 89
    choral singing 56
    history 91

Whiffenpoofs 11, 74, 96
whiteness 8, 84, 121, 132, 134
Winstead 2, 19, 66, 132
wokeness 51, 127

www.ingramcontent.com/pod-product-compliance
Lightning Source LLC
Chambersburg PA
CBHW070641300426
44111CB00013B/2211